A LITTLE GIANT® BOOK

SIDE-SPLITTERS

Joseph Rosenbloom
Illustrated by Sanford Hoffman & Joyce Behr

STERLING

New York / London
www.sterlingpublishing.com/kids

Library of Congress Cataloging-in-Publication Data

Rosenbloom, Joseph.
Little giant book of side-splitters/ Joseph Rosenbloom; illustrated by Sanford
Hoffman and Joyce Behr.
    p. cm.
ISBN 1-4027-2062-9
1. Wit and humor, Juvenile. I. Hoffman, Sanford. II Behr, Joyce. III. Title.

PN6166.R79 2005
818'.5402--dc22

                                                        2005010890

Lot#: 10   9   8   7   6   5   4   3
09/11

Published by Sterling Publishing Co., Inc.
387 Park Avenue South, New York, NY 10016
Material in this book previously appeared in *Get Well Quick! Jokes and Riddles* ©
1989, *How Do You Make an Elephant Laugh?* © 1979, *Looniest Limerick Book in
the World* © 1982, *Mad Scientist* © 1982, *Monster Madness* © 1980, and *Wacky
Insults and Terrible Jokes* © 1983. Artwork © by Joyce Behr and Sanford Hoffman.
Distributed in Canada by Sterling Publishing
c/o Canadian Manda Group, 165 Dufferin Street
Toronto, Ontario, Canada M6K 3H6
Distributed in the United Kingdom by GMC Distribution Services,
Castle Place, 166 High Street, Lewes, East Sussex, England BN7 1XU
Distributed in Australia by Capricorn Link (Australia) Pty. Ltd.
P.O. Box 704, Windsor, NSW 2756, Australia

Printed in China
All rights reserved

Sterling ISBN-13: 978-1-4027-4975-9
        ISBN-10: 1-4027-4975-9

For information about custom editions, special sales, premium and
corporate purchases, please contact Sterling Special Sales
Department at 800-805-5489 or specialsales@sterlingpub.com.

Contents

1

That's Ridiculous!

What does a mechanical frog say?
   "Robot, robot!"

What's green and jumps three feet every five seconds?
   A frog with hiccups.

How do you make an elephant laugh?
   Tickle its ivories.

How can you tell an elephant from spaghetti?

The elephant doesn't slip off the end of your fork.

What kind of geese are found in Portugal?

Portu-geese.

Criss Cross

What would you get if you crossed . . .

. . . a porcupine with a sheep?

An animal that knits its own sweaters.

. . . chocolate and a sheep?

A Hershey baaa.

. . . a sheep and a banana?
  A baa-nana.

. . . a ballpoint pen and a hippopotamus?
  The Ink-credible Hulk.

What do geese get when they eat too much chocolate?
  Goose pimples.

What do you get if you blow your hair dryer down a rabbit hole?
  Hot cross bunnies.

What's green and has two legs and a trunk?
  A seasick tourist.

What's a monster's normal eyesight?
  20-20-20-20-20.

How does a monster count to eighteen?
  On its fingers.

What do ghosts chew?
  Booble gum.

When do comedians take milk and sugar?
  At tea-hee time.

What cuts lawns and gives milk?
  A lawn moo-er.

Say These Three Times Quickly

The Abominable Snowman seeks six thick sticks.

Mummies munch much mush;
Monsters munch much mush;
Many mummies and monsters
Must munch much mush.

Should a shark share swordfish steak?

Should a sheep shave a short single shingle thin, or shave a short thin single cedar shingle thinner?

Where does the gingerbread man sleep?
Under a cookie sheet.

What weighs two tons, feels cold to the touch, and comes on a stick?
A hippopopsicle.

What clothing does a house wear?
Address.

What do you get when you use soap and water on the stove?
Foam on the range.

What did the duck say when it finished shopping?

"Just put it on my bill."

What game do baby chickens play?

Peck-a-boo.

When is it good manners to spit in a man's face?

When his mustache is on fire.

If lightning strikes an orchestra, who's most likely to get hit?

The conductor.

What's yellow and goes "hmmmm"?

An electric lemon.

What's long and yellow and always points north?

A magnetic banana.

2

Loony Limericks: Now You Know

No matter how grouchy you're feeling
You'll find that a limerick is healing.
  It grows like a wreath
  All around the front teeth,
Thus preserving the face from
    congealing.

There was an old fellow of Cosham
Who took out his false teeth to
    wash 'em.
  But his wife said, "Now, Jack,
  If you don't put them back,
I'll jump on those old things and
    squash 'em."

There once was a sailor named Link
Whose mates rushed him off to the
    clink.
  Said he, "I've a skunk
  As a pet in my bunk—
That's no reason for raising a stink."

There was a man in Atchison
Whose trousers had rough patches on.
  He found them great,
  He'd often state,
To scratch his wooden matches on.

There was a young lady of
      Twickenham
Whose boots were too tight to walk
      quick in 'em.
  She wore them awhile
  But after a mile,
She pulled them both off and was sick
      in 'em.

There was an old widower, Doyle,
Who wrapped his late wife in tinfoil.
  He thought it would please her
  To stay in the freezer——
And, anyway, outside she'd spoil.

To a person arriving in Heaven
Said St. Peter, "We dine sharp at seven,
  Then breakfast's at eight—
  Never mind if you're late—
'Cause there's biscuits and milk at
    eleven."

Said a cellist, a modest young fellow,
When praised for his playing so
    mellow,
  "It's the easiest thing;
  I just butter each string
With a spoonful of strawberry Jell-O."

The girl in the Chinese pagoda
Ate onions from fair Minnesota,
   And garlic from Greece
   And Limburger cheese
And her friends dropped like flies
    from the odor.

There was a longshoreman named Sid
Who ate sixty-five eggs in Madrid.
   When they asked, "Are you faint?"
   He replied, "No, I ain't,
But I don't feel as well as I did."

3

Doctor, Doctor!

Why do surgeons wear masks during operations?
So that if they make a mistake, no one will know who did it.

What kind of doctor operates on Styrofoam?

A *plastic surgeon.*

Tell the Doctor

PATIENT: Will you treat me?

DOCTOR: Absolutely not! You'll have to pay like everyone else.

PATIENT: Doctor, Doctor, I swallowed a spoon!

DOCTOR: Well, sit down and don't stir.

PATIENT: Doctor, Doctor, I swallowed a knife and fork!

DOCTOR: Well, I guess you'll have to eat with your fingers.

PATIENT: Doctor, Doctor, I swallowed a roll of film!

DOCTOR: Well, don't worry. Nothing serious will develop.

WOMAN: Doctor, Doctor, my little boy has swallowed a bullet! What should I do?

DOCTOR: Well, don't point him at anybody.

DOCTOR: What's your problem?

PATIENT: I like bow ties.

DOCTOR: Is that all? Thousands of people like bow ties. I prefer them myself.

PATIENT: You do? What a relief! How do you like them, boiled or fried?

REPORTER: Doctor, what's the best thing to do when your ear rings?
DOCTOR: Answer it.

DOCTOR: You have a condition called "Updoc."
PATIENT: What's "Updoc"?
DOCTOR: Nothing much. What's up with you?

DOCTOR: About this habit of talking to yourself—it's nothing to worry about.
PATIENT: Well, maybe not, but I'm such an awful bore.

PATIENT: Doctor, Doctor, come quickly! I've swallowed my fountain pen!
DOCTOR: What are you doing in the meantime?
PATIENT: Using a pencil.

Seeing Spots

"I've been seeing spots before my eyes lately."
"Have you seen a doctor?"
"No, just spots."

NIT: The doctor finally cured me of seeing spots.
NAT: How did she do that?
NIT: She took away my dominoes.

"I went to the eye doctor because I kept seeing spots. He gave me glasses."
"Did the glasses help?"
"Oh, yes, now I can see the spots much better."

What do you have if your
head feels hot, your feet
are cold, and you see spots
in front of your eyes?

You probably have a
polka dot sock over
your head.

"Doctor, Doctor, my eyesight
is getting worse!"
    "You're absolutely right. This is the post
office."

DOCTOR: Have your eyes ever been
    checked?
PATIENT: No, they've always been plain
    brown.

Why is an eye doctor like a teacher?
    Both of them test the pupils.

What do eye doctors sing when they test you?

"Oh, say can you see . . ."

What did Old MacDonald see on the eye chart?

E-I-E-I-O.

Where is the best place to build offices for opticians and optometrists?

On a site for sore eyes.

PATIENT: Can I sleep in my contact lenses?
DOCTOR: No, your feet would stick out.

Making a Spectacle of Yourself

"You need glasses," said the eye doctor.

"But I'm already wearing glasses," said the patient.

"In that case," said the doctor, "I need glasses."

Did you hear about the doctor who fell into a lens-grinding machine and made a spectacle of himself?

EYE DOCTOR: There now, with the glasses you'll be able to read everything.
WILLIE: Hurray! You mean I don't have to go to school anymore?

Notice in the Want Ads

LOST: THICK-LENS READING GLASSES. FINDER, PLEASE ADVERTISE IN LARGE PRINT.

Why did the doctor pour oil on his hands?
He wanted to be a smooth operator.

What does a polite surgeon say when he is about to operate?

"May I cut in?"

What did the man do when he found Chicago, Ill?

He called Baltimore, MD.

DOCTOR: Sorry I made you wait so long.
PATIENT: I didn't mind the wait so much, but I did think you'd like to treat my illness in its early stages.

DOCTOR: Ouch! Ouch!
WOMAN: Junior, please say
"ah" so the nice doctor
can take her finger out of
your mouth.

> Knock-knock.
> *Who's there?*
> Agatha.
> *Agatha who?*
> Agatha cold.

NURSE: Why is Tommy sticking his tongue
out at me?
WOMAN: Sorry. I guess the doctor forgot to
tell him to put it back in.

What's the most educated instrument?
*A thermometer, because it has so many
degrees.*

A maiden at college, Miss Keyes,
Weighed down by BAs and MDs,
 Collapsed from the strain
 Said her doctor, "It's plain
You are killing yourself—by degrees!"

An Apple a Day

An apple a day keeps the doctor away—if it's aimed right.

If an apple a day keeps the doctor away, what does an onion a day do?
 It keeps everybody away.

Ask the Doctor

PATIENT: Doctor, Doctor, I was playing a harmonica and I swallowed it!

DOCTOR: Lucky you weren't playing a piano.

PATIENT: Doctor, Doctor, I swallowed a clock last week!

DOCTOR: Good grief, why did you wait so long to come to see me?

PATIENT: I didn't want to alarm you.

PATIENT: Doctor, Doctor, my stomach hurts!

DOCTOR: Stop bellyaching!

BILLY: My father has been in a hospital for years.

GILLY: That's terrible. What's the matter with him?

BILLY: Nothing. He's a doctor.

PATIENT: Doctor, Doctor, I have carrots growing out of my ears!
DOCTOR: How did that happen?
PATIENT: I have no idea. I planted potatoes.

How long should doctors practice medicine?
Until they get it right.

NURSE (on telephone): Mr. Jones, you haven't paid your bill in two months and the doctor is very upset.
MR. JONES: Well, tell him to take two aspirins and call me in the morning.

What is a foot doctor's favorite song?
"There's No Business Like Toe Business."

What kind of X rays do foot doctors take?
Foot-ographs.

4
Monster Mash

How did the mad
scientist get rid of
flies in his
laboratory?
*He hired a good
outfielder.*

What kind of mistakes do ghosts make?
Boo-boos.

Did you hear what happened to the ghoul
who fell down the well?
He kicked the bucket.

What kind of ant is ten feet tall?
 A *gi-ant*.

What do you get when a giant walks
through a potato field?
 Mashed potatoes.

What do you get when a giant walks
through your vegetable garden?
 Squash.

Criss Cross

What would you get if you crossed . . .

. . . a monster and a chicken?
A creature that's always in a fowl mood.

. . . a monster and a goat?
A creature that eats a path to your door.

. . . peanut butter, bread, jelly, and a werewolf?
A hairy peanut butter and jelly sandwich that howls when the moon is full.

What skeleton was a master detective?
Sherlock Bones.

What's a demon's favorite dessert?
Devil's food cake.

What's small, lives underground, and solves crimes?

Sherlock Gnomes.

Why is the letter G scary?

Because it turns a host into a ghost.

What is a zombie's favorite stone?

A tombstone.

How do zombies speak?

In a grave voice.

What's the Difference?

What's the difference between a monster and peanut butter?

A monster doesn't stick to the roof of your mouth.

What's the difference between zombies and darned socks?

One is dead men, the other is men-ded.

What's the difference between a kangaroo and a mummy?

One bounds around, the other is bound around.

What color is a ghost?

Boo!

What is a ghost's favorite thing on a farm?

The scarecrow.

What did the skeleton say when it got a comb for its birthday?

"I'll never part with it."

What do you call the expression on a zombie's face?
  Deadpan.

Do zombies enjoy being dead?
  Of corpse! Of corpse!

What does the hangman read every morning?
  The noosepaper.

What do you call the sweetheart of a ghoul?
  A ghoul friend.

What kind of keys open a tomb?
  Skeleton keys.

What kind of raincoat does a ghoul wear on a rainy day?
  A wet one.

What is purple and eats people?
A *purple people eater.*

What do you call a skeleton that doesn't like to work?
Lazybones.

Mad About Martians

What did the Martian say when he landed
in a field of weeds?
"Take me to your weeder."

How do Martians drink their tea?
From flying saucers.

What's soft, white, and comes from Mars?
Martian-mallows.

Two Martians landed on a corner with a traffic light.

"I saw her first," one Martian said.

"So what?" said the other. "I'm the one she winked at."

〜〜〜

What do monsters drink during warm weather?

Ice-ghoul lemonade.

What do you do with a green monster?

Wait until he ripens.

What part of you moves when you dream about a ghoul?

Your flesh—it crawls.

What's a ghoul's favorite vegetable juice?

Tomb-ato juice.

What's the first thing you put in a
graveyard?
   Your feet.

What newspaper did the dinosaurs read?
   The Prehistoric Times.

How can you tell if there's a giant in your
sandwich?
   It's hard to lift.

How do you make a monster stew?
Keep it waiting for two hours.

How many ghouls can fit into an empty casket?
One. After that the casket isn't empty anymore.

When do you charge a Frankenstein monster?
When he can't pay cash.

Why did the monster chase its tail?
It was trying to make both ends meet.

Who writes books about haunted houses?
Ghostwriters.

What has twenty heads but can't think?
A book of matches.

How do you cut a dinosaur in two?
  With a dino-saw.

What kind of tests do they give you in witch school?
  Hex-aminations.

Who belongs to the monsters' PTA?
  Mummies and deadies.

What do you eat for supper when a
haunted house burns down?
  Roast ghost.

How do ghosts eat food?
  By gobblin' it.

What did the big ghost say to the little
ghost when they entered the car?
  "Fasten your sheet belt."

What should you watch when you're
talking to an angry monster?
  Your step.

Why was the gravedigger so well liked?
  Because he was such a down-to-earth guy.

Is it all right to eat pickles with your fingers?

No, eat the pickles first—then eat your fingers.

What did the mother ghost say to the baby ghost?

"It's not polite to spook until you are spooken to."

What do you say when you meet a two-headed monster?

"Hello, hello!"

How do you treat a sick monster?

With respect.

What do you call a monster who eats his mother and father?

An orphan.

What do you call a clean, nice,
hardworking, friendly monster?
  A failure.

What do you do with a blue monster?
  Cheer him up.

5

School Days

The telephone rang in the office of the school principal. "Hello, may I speak to the principal, please?"

"This is the principal."

"I'm calling to say that my son cannot come to school today because he has a bad cold."

"Who is this speaking, please?"

"This is my father."

"Mom, I can't go to school today. I sprained my ankle."

"Of all the lame excuses!"

TEACHER: Johnny, can you tell me what they did at the Boston Tea Party?

JOHNNY: I don't know, Teacher. I wasn't invited.

What's the most important thing to remember in chemistry class?

Don't lick the spoon!

What's the best way to pass a geometry test?

Know all the angles.

Why did the teacher excuse the little
firefly?
*Because when you've got to glow, you've
got to glow.*

There was an old teacher, Miss May,
Whose brain had begun to give way.
    Pupils' names she forgot,
    But that bothered her not,
For she simply addressed them as
        "Hey!"

Said a boy to his teacher
        one day,
"Wright has not written
        'rite' right, I say!"
    And the teacher replied
    As the error she eyed:
"Right!—Wright, write 'rite' right,
        right away!"

TEACHER: What's a vacuum, William?
WILLIAM: Wait a minute, Teacher. I have it in my head.

What's the best way to cut down on pollution in schools?
Use unleaded pencils.

Funny History

What kind of illumination did Noah use on the ark?
Floodlights.

What mouse was ruler of the Romans?
Julius Cheeser.

What did you need to win a race in the old Roman Colosseum?
Faith, hope, and chariot.

Why didn't Sir Isaac Newton trust the Law of Gravity?
Because it always let him down.

What ship brought the first horses to America?
The Hayflower.

What famous American gave King George III a headache?
Thomas Paine.

Who helped invent the telephone and had a cookie named after him?
Alexander Graham Cracker.

What did Mrs. Revere say to her husband?
"I don't care who's coming, Paul. It's my turn to use the horse!"

What was the patriot's reply when Paul Revere asked him to join the fight against the British?

"Give me a minute, man, and I'll be with you."

What counterfeiters were active during the American Revolution?

The Valley Forgers.

How did the patriots in the American Revolution guard their secrets?

By not telling Tories.

What was Samuel Langhorne Clemens's pen name?

He never had a name for his pen.

What were Alexander Graham Bell's first words?

"Goo-goo."

A tutor who tooted a flute
Tried to teach two young tooters to
     toot.
  Said the two to the tutor,
  "Is it harder to toot, or
To tutor two tooters to toot?"

TEACHER: What are nitrates?
BILLY: What you pay for a telephone call after five P.M.

TEACHER: What is mean temperature?
SUZY: Twenty degrees below zero when you don't have long underwear.

What kind of beat do math teachers like to dance to?
Logarithms.

Rocks in Your Head

What does an astronaut do when he gets dirty?
He takes a meteor shower.

What's a geologist's favorite dessert?
Marble cake.

What sweet do geologists like?
Rock candy.

FIRST GEOLOGIST: I bet you ten dollars that my name is harder than yours.

SECOND GEOLOGIST: Okay. What's your name?

FIRST GEOLOGIST: Sam Stone. Your name can't be harder than that. I win.

SECOND GEOLOGIST: No, you don't. My name is George B. Harder.

Whose fault will it be if California falls into the ocean?
  San Andreas'.

Where do geologists go to relax?
  Rock concerts.

What is a geologist's favorite lullaby?
   "Rock-a-Bye Baby."

How do you make notes out of stone?
   Rearrange the letters.

What does a geologist have for breakfast?
   Rock and roll.

What kind of music do you hear when you throw a stone into the lake?
   Plunk rock.

When are geologists unpopular?
When they are faultfinders.

When are geologists unhappy?
When people take them for granite.

What do archaeologists talk about when they get together?
The good old days.

Criss Cross

What would you get if you crossed . . .

. . . a bag of cement, a stone, and a radio?
Hard rock music.

. . . an earthquake and a forest fire?
Shake and Bake.

. . . a stone and a shark?
Rockjaw.

. . . a chicken and a cement truck?
A hen that lays sidewalks.

6

Wacky Insults: Quacking Up

"It seems to me I've seen your face
somewhere before."

"How odd."

"Yes, it certainly is."

"I suppose you think I'm a perfect idiot."
   "No, no one is perfect."

"I have an idea."
   "Your luck is improving."

No one can fool you—you're too ignorant.

Use tact—fathead!

What you lack in intelligence, you make up for in stupidity.

"Did you fill in that blank yet?"
   "What blank?"
   "The one between your ears."

"I'm sorry I lost my head."
   "Well, don't worry about it. You still have the other one."

"Can you tell when someone is lying?"
   "Yes, usually."
   "Well, allow me to say it's been a pleasure meeting you."

"When I was young, my mother used to say that if I made ugly faces, my face would stay that way forever."
   "She was right."

"Why don't you answer me?"

"I did. I shook my head."

"You don't expect me to hear it rattle from here, do you?"

Are you really leaving or are you only trying to brighten my day?

Why don't you do like a locomotive and make tracks?

"Please call me a taxi."

"Okay, you're a taxi. But to tell you the truth, you look more like a truck."

"Did you fall down the elevator shaft?"

"No, I was just sitting here and they built it around me."

"I guess we all just live and learn."
　"No, you just live."

"How are you doing?"
　"As well as can be expected."
　"Pretty bad, eh?"

"What did you have in mind?"
　"Nothing."
　"Ah, as usual, I see."

"What time is it?"
　"Sorry, but my watch is on the bum."
　"I know that—but what time is it?"

May I Help You?

"The way you dress will never go out of style."

"Why, thank you."

"It will look just as terrible ten years from now."

"I just came from the beauty parlor."

"What's the matter, weren't they open?"

"You shouldn't make fun of my looks. All human beings are made in the same mold."

"Yes, but some are moldier than others."

"I'd like to find a dress to match my eyes."

"Sorry, we don't carry bloodshot dresses."

"Have you any scarves to match my eyes?"

"No, but we have soft hats to match your head."

"I didn't come here to be insulted."

"Oh? Where do you usually go?"

"I earn a living by my wits."

"Well, half a living is better than none."

"I'm not myself today."

"Yes, and I noticed the improvement right away."

"I used to think . . ."
  "What made you stop?"

"What nice hands you have."
  "My hands are soft because I wear gloves at night."
  "And do you also sleep with your hat on?"

"I've played the piano for years—on and off."
  "What was the problem—slippery stool?"

 You remind me of yesterday's coffee—bitter and cold.

You are living proof that wisdom doesn't come with age.

Why don't you go back to where you came from—if they'll still take you?

"I just flew in from Europe."

"Your arms must be tired."

"Someone once told me always to be myself."

"Well, you couldn't have gotten worse advice."

"Was your boss angry when you told him you were going to quit next week?"

"He sure was. He thought it was this week."

"My fiancé says I'm the prettiest and most interesting girl he's ever met."

"And you'll trust yourself for life to a liar like that?"

Your face reminds me of a movie star—
Lassie.

"I can trace my ancestors all the way back
to royalty."
    "King Kong?"

"Who do you think you're talking to?"
    "How many guesses do I get?"

"Do you think I'm a fool?"
    "No, but what's my opinion against
thousands of others?"

"Don't you think I look like a slender
birch?"
    "No, you look more like a knotty pine."

"I remember when I was a mere child . . ."
    "Wow, what a memory!"

Why don't you go to a tailor and have a fit?

"Whenever I'm in the dumps, I buy new clothes."
  "So—that's where you get them!"

Your clothes are so loud, they should come with a volume control.

"When is feeding time at the zoo?"
"One o'clock. If you hurry, you can still get a bite."

"Good-bye."
"You've already said good-bye twice."
"It's always a pleasure to say good-bye to you."

7

Loony Limericks: How Absurd!

A fellow who lived on the Rhine
Saw some fish on which he wished to
   dine.
  But how to invite them?
  He said, "I will write them!"
He sat down and dropped them a line.

There was a young lady named Lee
Who swam all alone in the sea.
   People said, "You'll be drowned,"
   But she sniffed and she frowned,
And said, "Pish-tosh and fiddle-de-
      dee!"

At the zoo I remarked to an emu,
"I cannot pretend I esteem you.
   You're a greedy old bird,
   And your walk is absurd,
And not even your feathers redeem
      you."

There was an old lady of Reading
Who never knew where she was
      heading.
   She'd start in the east
   On her way to a feast,
And end in the north at a wedding.

Two eager and dashing young beaus
Were held up and robbed of their
    clothes.
  While the weather is hot,
  They don't mind it a lot,
But what will they do when it snows?

Said a crow to a pelican, "Grant
Me the loan of your bill, for my aunt
   Has asked me to tea."
   Said the other, "Not me,
Ask my brother, please, this pelican't!"

A woman named Mary McGowen
Once said to her old husband, "How
      in
   The world can I wear
   My new hat to the fair
If you've used it for milking the cow
      in?"

An athletic young girl of Papua
Invited a bull to pursue her.
   She vaulted the gate
   Just a fraction too late;
Now when she laughs, she says, "Oo-
      ah!"

8

Sick Sick Sick

What would happen if you swallowed a dress?

You'd have a frock in your throat.

PATIENT: The enemy sent a top secret message, but I was able to read it.

DOCTOR: Top secret? How did you decipher it?

PATIENT: Easy. I had a code in the head.

Why Did They See the Doctor?

Why did the chicken see the doctor?
It had people pox.

Why did the banana see the doctor?
It wasn't peeling well.

Why did the dog see the doctor?
Because a stitch in time saves canine.

Why did the math book see the doctor?
It had problems.

Why did the outlaw see the doctor?
He was a sick shooter.

PATIENT: Doctor, Doctor, every bone in my
body hurts!
DOCTOR: Be grateful you're not a sardine!

What animal do you feel like when you
have a fever?
A little otter.

What's in a Sneeze?

How does a tennis player sneeze?
  "A tennis-shoe! A tennis-shoe!"

How does Sherlock Holmes sneeze?
  "A clue! A clue!"

> Knock-knock.
>   *Who's there?*
> Stan.
>   *Stan who?*
> Stan back. I'm going to sneeze!

78

What's the difference between a person with a cold and a strong wind?
One blows a sneeze; the other blows a breeze.

Where does a sneeze usually point?
At-you!

What kind of paper is most like a sneeze?
A tissue.

What should you do when an elephant sneezes?
Get out of the way.

Knock-knock.
Who's there?
Hutch.
Hutch who?
Gesundheit!

What should you say when the Statue of
Liberty sneezes?
  "God bless America."

What is red, white, and blue and
convenient to have on hand when you
sneeze?
  A hanky doodle dandy.

What happens when corn catches cold?
  It gets an earache.

Did you hear about the cowboy whose voice was so hoarse that they put a saddle on it?

What sickness can't you talk about until it's cured?
  Laryngitis.

> A fellow from Nome with a cough
> Would snicker and snortle and scoff
>   At warm woolen drawers
>   When going outdoors—
> 'Twas pneumonia that carried him off.

What kind of alligator do you find in a hospital?
  An illigator.

DOCTOR: Your cough sounds better today.
PATIENT: It should. I practiced all night.

Doctor, Doctor

PATIENT: Doctor, Doctor, you've got to help me! My eyes are dripping like a faucet, my throat feels like a lead pipe, and my nose is all clogged up!
DOCTOR: Have you been to a plumber?

PATIENT: Doctor, Doctor, I work like a horse, eat like a bird, and I'm as tired as a dog!
DOCTOR: Have you been to a veterinarian?

PATIENT: Doctor, Doctor, what's the matter with me? Sometimes I think I'm a tepee and sometimes I think I'm a wigwam!
DOCTOR: Obviously, you're two tents.

PATIENT: Doctor, Doctor, I've only got fifty-nine seconds to live!
DOCTOR: Hold on, I'll be with you in a minute.

PATIENT: I've been fighting and fighting this cold and it won't go away.
DOCTOR: There's your mistake. Never fight a cold. That's what makes a cold sore.

How do you feel if you have a sore throat and fleas?
Hoarse and buggy.

DOCTOR: Please breathe out three times.

PATIENT: Is that so you can check my lungs?

DOCTOR: No, so I can clean my eyeglasses.

Health Best-sellers

Sports Injuries by Charlie Hawes & Aiken Bakke

Curing Poison Ivy by Don S. Crachit

Overeating by Belle E. Ake

First Aid by Justin Tyme

"Sam went to Arizona for his asthma."

"What's the matter—couldn't he get it here?"

Doctor, Doctor

PATIENT: Doctor, Doctor, I feel like an elephant!
DOCTOR: Tusk, tusk.

PATIENT: Doctor, Doctor, I feel like a sheep!
DOCTOR: That's too baa-d.

PATIENT: Doctor, Doctor, I feel like a canary!
DOCTOR: Don't worry. Your condition is tweet-able.

DARRYL: I went to a doctor and he told me that my liver is twenty inches long.

JEAN: Well, that shows you come from a line of long livers.

What's the Difference?

What's the difference between a cow with a sore throat and an angry crowd?

One moos badly, the other boos madly.

What's the difference between ammonia and pneumonia?

Ammonia comes in bottles; pneumonia comes in chests.

What's the difference between a photocopying machine and a virus?

One makes facsimiles; the other makes sick families.

What's the difference between a bus driver and a cold?

One knows the stops; the other stops the nose.

What's the difference between a dressmaker and a nurse?

One cuts the dresses; the other dresses the cuts.

9

Trick or Treat!

What should you do with a prune that's a year old?

Give it a birthday party.

What do canaries say on Halloween?
"Twick or tweet!"

What loses its head every morning but gets it back at night?
A pillow.

Why are rabbits underpaid?
Because they'll always work for a little celery.

What do you call a riot in the post office?
A stampede.

What comes out at night and goes "Flap! Flap! Chomp! Ouch!"?
A vampire with a sore tooth.

If a plumber works hard all day, what kind of dreams does he have at night?
Pipe dreams.

Criss Cross

What would you get if you crossed . . .

. . . a fifty-foot Martian and a three-hundred-pound chicken?

The biggest cluck in the solar system.

. . . a woodpecker and a lion?
An animal that knocks before it eats you.

. . . an octopus and a cow?
An animal that can milk itself.

. . . a porcupine and a skunk?
A pretty lonesome animal.

. . . a crocodile and a kangaroo?
Leaping lizards!

How many feet are there in a yard?
It depends on how many people are standing in the yard.

What person makes a living by talking to himself?
A ventriloquist.

What song does an electric cowboy sing?
  "Ohm on the Range."

What kind of toys does a psychiatrist's child play with?

Mental blocks.

How do you kiss a hockey player?

You pucker up.

By the Seashore

What doesn't get any wetter no matter how much it rains?

The ocean.

Why did the ocean roar at the ships?

Because they crossed it so many times.

Why was the ocean arrested?

Because it beat upon the shore.

An oyster from Kalamazoo
Confessed he was feeling quite blue.
  "For," said he, "as a rule,
  When the weather turns cool,
I'm apt to get into a stew."

There's a lady in Kalamazoo
Who bites her oysters in two;
  She has a misgiving,
  Should any be living,
They'd raise such a hullabaloo.

How do you cut the ocean in two?
With a sea-saw.

What do two oceans say when they meet after many years?
"Long time no sea."

What's the most romantic part of the ocean?

The spot where buoy meets gull.

What's a shark's favorite flavor of ice cream?

Sharkolate.

What character got all his work done by Friday?

Robinson Crusoe.

How did the ditchdigger get his job?
He just fell into it.

What do you find more in sorrow than in anger?
The letter R.

What makes a chess player happy?
Taking a knight off.

What happened to the woman who covered herself with vanishing cream?
Nobody knows.

What geometric figure do sailors fear?
The Bermuda Triangle.

What does an executioner do on his day off?
Nothing. He just hangs around.

Who do mermaids date?
They go out with the tide.

Why is a leaking faucet like a horse race?
It's off and running.

Where do nuts gather?
At the Hershey bar.

What kind of bars can't keep prisoners in jail?

Chocolate bars.

Did you hear the joke about the chocolate cake?

Never mind, it's too rich.

What would you get if you stacked thousands of pizza pies on top of each other?

A leaning tower of pizza.

What's a pizza's favorite means of transportation?

Pie-cycle.

Where do cows go for entertainment?

To the moooo-vies.

Say These Three Times Quickly

The glum ghoul grows glummer.

The haunted cheap chip shop sells cheap chips to haunted ships.

Frankenstein favors five free fruit floats.

Flo fled Bigfoot Friday.

"Six small slick seals," said the skeleton.

The witch bewitched the thin twin tinsmith.

Which witch bewitched which watch?

10

Games Monsters Play

What is a monster's favorite necklace?
A choker.

What was Dr. Jekyll's favorite game?
Hyde-and-seek.

What game do ghost children like to play?
Haunt-and-seek.

Sign in a Funeral Home

SATISFACTION GUARANTEED OR DOUBLE YOUR
MUMMY BACK

PING: Did you hear about the new
chocolate bar called Jaws?
PONG: No—what does it cost?
PING: An arm and a leg.

Did you hear about the monster who had
such a repulsive personality, when he
threw a boomerang it wouldn't come back?

Why did the giant jog every morning?
To get his extra-size.

Where does Dr. Jekyll go to get some privacy?

To his Hyde-away.

FLIP: Have you heard the joke about the witch's broom?

FLOP: No, I haven't.

FLIP: That's strange. It's sweeping the nation.

FIRST WITCH: I had to drop out of witch school.

SECOND WITCH: What happened?

FIRST WITCH: I flunked spelling.

If the stork brings human babies, who brings the giant babies?

Cranes.

Did Dr. Frankenstein amuse his monster?

Yes, he kept him in stitches.

Monster Best-sellers

Calming Werewolves by Justin
Casey Howells

The Space Invaders by Athena
Martian

Is There a Loch Ness Monster?
by Y. Knott

The Big Bang Theory
by Adam Balm

Reptiles Around the World
by Sally Mander

A visitor once to Loch Ness
Met the monster, who left him a mess.
   They returned his entrails
   By the regular mails
And the rest of the stuff by express.

Where do ghosts buy their sheets?
   In a boo-tique.

Criss Cross

What would you get if you crossed . . .

. . . a jolly fat man in a red suit with a werewolf?
   Santa Claws.

. . . a werewolf with a boat?
   A wolf in ship's clothing.

. . . a werewolf and a witch?
A mad dog that chases airplanes.

. . . a werewolf and a zebra?
A killer in a striped suit.

. . . a werewolf with Lassie?
A pedigreed monster.

. . . a pet dog and a werewolf?
A new owner every full moon.

Why are vampire families so close?
Because blood is thicker than water.

Why was the giant arrested when he set out on a trip?

Because he hit the road.

What keeps a monster from being a good dancer?

His three left feet.

When is a werewolf most likely to enter a house?
When the door is open.

Who won the monster beauty contest?
No one.

NIT: What's the difference between a monster and a matterbaby?
WIT: What's a "matterbaby"?
NIT: Nothing, sweetie. What's the matter with you?

How do you stop an angry monster from charging?
Take away his credit cards.

How can you tell when witches are carrying a time bomb?
You can hear their brooms tick.

If you were walking along a dark street and met a Frankenstein monster, a ghost, a werewolf, and a mummy, what should you do?

Hope it's Halloween.

If a werewolf lost his tail, where could he get another?

At a retail store.

Where does the Frankenstein monster go when he loses a hand?

To a secondhand store.

Why are skeletons like blank applications?

Because their forms have not been filled out.

What do you call a skeleton who's a good friend?

A bony crony.

What do monsters have that no one else has?

Baby monsters.

What do witches ring for in a hotel?

B-room service.

What do you call a group of zombie dancers?

A corpse de ballet.

What is dangerous, yellow, and hot?
  Shark-infested custard.

 Creature Features

How do you make a strawberry shake?
  Take it to a horror movie.

What do you say about a horrible mummy movie?
  "It sphinx!"

What would happen if a giant sat in front of you at the movies?
  You'd miss most of the film.

Where do ghouls like to sit when they go to the theater?
  Dead center.

IGOR: What is the plot of that new science
 fiction movie?
BORIS: It's the same old story: boy meets girl,
 boy loses girl, boy builds new girl . . .

FIRST UNDERTAKER: Poor Sam! He died from drinking shellac.
SECOND UNDERTAKER: Well, at least he had a fine finish.

When the executioner registered at the hotel, the clerk asked him what kind of room he desired. The executioner explained. "My needs are small. I just want a place to hang my hat and a few friends."

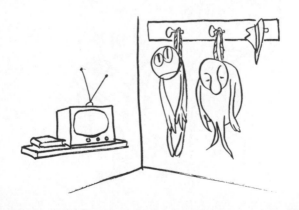

Where do supernatural creatures live?
  In ghost towns.

How did they ship skeletons in the Old West?
  By bony express.

How does a dinosaur get to Carnegie Hall?
  By practicing his scales.

What resembles the Blob and has chrome stripes?
  The deluxe Blob.

NIT: Did you hear about the monster rip-off?
WIT: No. What did they rip off?
NIT: Arms, legs, heads . . .

How far can you walk into a cemetery?
  Only halfway. After that, you're walking out.

Why was the werewolf hired by the radio station?

Because he had the paws for station identification.

What happened to the wolf who fell into the washing machine?

He became a wash-and-werewolf.

It's a lovely summer evening and Johnny and Sue are parked on a hill overlooking town. Johnny turns to Sue and says, "Sue, sweetheart, I have some good news and some bad news. The good news is that at any moment we can see a lovely full moon rise over the hill."

"Oh, you're so romantic," Sue says. "What is the bad news?"

"I'm a werewolf! Aaargh!"

11

Wacky Insults: Karate Chops

"Say, who do you think you're shoving?"
"I don't know—what's your name?"

"I'm a self-made man."
"I accept your apology."

You're so nervous, you keep coffee awake.

If I had a lower IQ, I might enjoy this conversation.

Nuts to You

"What's your name?"
    "Pistachio."
    "Pistachio! What kind of name is that?"
    "That's Pistachio to my friends—and nuts to you!"

"The mosquitoes are biting me."
    "Those aren't mosquitoes—those are gnats."
    "All right—mosquitoes to me—and gnats to you!"

"That boat does twenty miles an hour."

"Not twenty miles. You mean knots."

"Okay, miles to me—and knots to you!"

"I dreamed about zeros last night."

"You don't mean zeros, you mean naughts."

"Okay, zeroes to me—and naughts to you!"

"My great-grandfather fought with General Lee, my grandfather fought with the British, and my father fought with the Americans."

"Your family can't get along with anybody, can they?"

There's a good reason why you think the world is against you—it is.

Your little mind must be lonesome, rolling around in such an empty head.

119

"I throw myself into everything I do."

"Why don't you go out and find a deep hole?"

When I look at you, I wonder what Mother Nature had in mind.

"If I had a face like yours, I'd put it on a wall and throw a brick at it."

"If I had a face like yours, I'd put it on a brick and throw a wall at it."

You're so stupid, you think you have to stand on your head to turn things over in your mind.

Why don't you make like a ball and roll away?

Why don't you take a deep breath—and blow?

I can't figure out what makes you tick, but I think it's a time bomb.

"I always aim to tell the truth."
    "Bad shot, aren't you?"

You could go out of your mind and no one would know the difference.

"You must be a terrific bowler."
    "How did you know?"
    "I could tell by your pinhead."

"Would you like to travel to unknown places?"

"Yes, I would."

"Fine, go get lost."

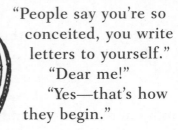

"People say you're so conceited, you write letters to yourself."

"Dear me!"

"Yes—that's how they begin."

The next time you get a toupee, get one with brains.

"What would you say if I asked you to marry me?"

"Nothing. I can't talk and laugh at the same time."

"Have you told your little boy not to go around imitating me?"

"Yes, I have. I told him not to act like an idiot."

You're all wrapped up in yourself—and you make a pretty small package.

You think you're a big cheese—but you only smell like one.

"You should put a sign on your head."

"What kind of sign?"

"VACANT."

"She's so stuck up. She thinks she's so much better than me."

"Why, that conceited, good-for-nothing moron! You're certainly every bit as good as she is!"

I dreamt about you last night. Worst nightmare I ever had.

"I learned to play the piano in no time."
"Yes, and it sounds that way, too."

"I've been playing the piano for five years."
"Aren't your fingers tired?"

The last time I saw a mouth like yours, it had a fishhook in it.

"You're half an hour late. I've been standing here like a fool."
"I can't help how you stand."

The only thing you can keep in your head for more than an hour is a cold.

"How are you?"
  "Wonderful."
  "I'm glad someone thinks so."

The more I think of you—
the less I think of you.

I've seen more
interesting faces on
clocks.

You hold your nose so
high in the air, there's
always an inch of snow on it.

Your problem is that you're always trying
to save both faces.

Things could be worse. You could be here
in person.

Some people are born great, some achieve greatness—you just grate.

You ought to be an auto racer—you're such a big drag.

Whatever is eating you must be suffering from indigestion.

You could make a fortune renting out your head as a balloon.

"If you work hard, you'll get ahead."
   "No, thanks, I already have a head."

If they're not talking about you, you're not listening.

You have an even disposition—always rotten.

"Only fools make absolute statements."
   "Are you sure of that?"
   "Absolutely!"

"Before I do anything, I stop to think."
   "The trouble is, you always forget to
start again."

"Am I boring you?"
   "No, just wake
me when you're
finished."

My house is
located near a lake.
Drop in sometime.

12

Monkey Business

WOMAN: Doctor, Doctor, you've got to help my son! All he does is scratch himself and swing from a tree.

DOCTOR: Don't worry, he's probably just going through a phase.

WOMAN: Oh, thank you, Doctor. How much do I owe you?

DOCTOR: Thirty bananas.

There was an old man of Khartoum
Who kept a baboon in his room.
   "It reminds me," he said,
   "Of a friend who is dead."
But he would never tell us of whom.

The menagerie came to our place
And I loved the gorilla's grimace.
   It surprised me to learn
   That he owned the concern,
Being human, but odd in the face.

King of the Jungle

If King Kong were attacked by an army, how would he fight back?
   With gorilla warfare.

Why does King Kong watch everything he says and does?
   Because he doesn't want to make a monkey of himself.

Knock-knock!
Who's there?
King Kong.
King Kong who?
"King Kong, the witch is dead . . ."

What do you say to King Kong when he gets married?
Kongratulations!

What's the best way to raise King Kong?
With a jack.

What is King Kong's favorite flower?
Chimp-pansies.

What should you do if you meet King Kong?
Give him a big banana.

How can you tell King Kong from a banana?
The banana is yellow.

What's the best way to take down a monkey's voice?
With an ape recorder.

What do you call a two-thousand-pound gorilla?

"Sir."

What's the best thing to do if you find a gorilla in your bed?

Sleep somewhere else.

What do you call a gorilla with cotton in his ears?

Anything you want. He can't hear you.

What kind of tool do you use to fix a broken gorilla?

A monkey wrench.

What did the monkey say when his sister had a baby?

"Well, I'll be a monkey's uncle!"

What song do gorillas sing in the spring?
"Ape-ril in Paris . . ."

What kind of apes grow on vines?
Gray apes.

How do you get to the Planet of the Apes?
By banana boat.

Criss Cross

What would you get if you crossed . . .

. . . an old car and a gorilla?
  A grease monkey.

. . . King Kong with a kangaroo?
  Big holes all over Australia.

. . . King Kong and a parrot?
  A lot of big talk.

Said a monk, as he swung by his tail,
To the little monks, female and male:
  "From your offspring, my dears,
  In not so many years,
May evolve a professor at Yale!"

13

Next!

Knock-knock.
   Who's there?
Amnesia.
   Amnesia who?
I see you have it too!

"Doctor, Doctor, I feel warm and out of breath!"

"You must have flu."

"No, I walked over."

When was medicine first mentioned in the Bible?

When Moses received the two tablets

Doctor, Doctor

WOMAN: Doctor, Doctor, you've got to help my son! He bites his nails in school.

DOCTOR: Lots of children bite their nails.

WOMAN: Their toenails?

WOMAN: Doctor, Doctor, you've got to help my son! He does bird imitations.

DOCTOR: Lots of people do bird imitations.

WOMAN: They eat worms?

What does a nurse measure that has no length, width, or thickness?
Your temperature.

What does a doctor do with a sick zeppelin?
He tries to helium.

"I'm the doctor's nurse."
  "Oh, is the doctor sick?"

Where do they send sick socks?
  To the hose-pital.

RIP: Those nurses are in training.
DIP: Really? Who are they going to fight?

PATIENT: The first thirty minutes that I'm
  up every morning, I feel dizzy. What
  should I do?
DOCTOR: Get up half an hour later.

DOCTOR: What happened to your thumb?
PATIENT: I hit the wrong nail.

PATIENT: I have a splinter in my finger.
DOCTOR: That's what you get for scratching
  your head.

Health Best-sellers

The Causes of Itching by Miss Kito Byte

Do You Need Surgery? by Noah I. L. Waite

The Secrets of Long Life by Sir Vival

You Can Be Healthy by Colin D. Head

Healthy Living by Vida Mynn

Successful Dieting by Yukon Dewitt & Troy Hodder

NURSE: Your pulse is as steady as a clock.
PATIENT: You've got your hand on my
    watch.

Why did the mother owl take her baby to
the doctor?
    Because it didn't give a hoot.

Why did the mother cow go to the doctor?
She felt udderly exhausted.

Why did the mother skunk take her baby
to the doctor?
Because it was out of odor.

Why did the mother cow take her baby to
the doctor?
Because it was so moo-dy.

141

What do you give an elk with indigestion?
  Elk-a-Seltzer.

What did the farmer use to cure his sick
hog?
  Oinkment.

Knock-knock.
  Who's there?
Avocado.
  Avocado who?
Avocado cold and dat's why I talk
dis way.

Doctor, Doctor

WOMAN: Doctor, Doctor, my husband thinks he's a refrigerator!

DOCTOR: If that's his only problem, don't worry about it.

WOMAN: But he sleeps with his mouth open and the light keeps me up all night!

WOMAN: Doctor, Doctor, my husband thinks he's an elevator!

DOCTOR: I'll look at him. Send him up.

WOMAN: I can't. He doesn't stop at your floor.

PATIENT: I don't think the pills you gave me arc doing me any good.

DOCTOR: Have you been taking them on an empty stomach?

PATIENT: I try, but they keep rolling off.

Although she had laryngitis, the woman protested loudly against the doctor's bill. "You charged fifty dollars," she complained, "and all you did was paint my throat!"

"What did you expect?" the doctor replied. "Wallpaper?"

DOCTOR: Did you follow my directions: Drink water thirty minutes before going to bed?

PATIENT: I tried to. But I was full after drinking for five minutes!

When they take out your appendix, they call it an appendectomy. When they take out your tonsils, they call it a tonsillectomy. What do they call it when they remove a growth from your head?

A *haircut.*

DOCTOR: Did you follow my directions?
PATIENT: Yes, Doctor. I've been taking three baths a day.
DOCTOR: Three what?
PATIENT: Three baths—just like the instructions on the bottle said.
DOCTOR: There must be some mistake.
PATIENT: Well, the bottle said to take a spoonful three times a day in water.

Why do many mummies have high blood pressure?

Because they're so wound up.

DOCTOR: The best time to take this medicine is just before retiring.

PATIENT: You mean I don't have to take it until I'm sixty-five years old?

PATIENT: I hear you are the greatest expert in the world at curing baldness. If you cure me, I'll give you anything you ask.

DOCTOR (after examining the patient): I have some good news and some bad news. The bad news is that I can't grow any more hair on your head. Now for the good news: I can shrink your head to fit the hair you've got.

PATIENT: My hair is coming out pretty fast. Can you give me something to keep it in?

DOCTOR: Sure. Here's an empty box.

DOCTOR: You've been my patient for ten years, Mr. Johnson. Why did you think I wouldn't recognize you?

MR. JOHNSON: Because I'm not myself today.

PATIENT: Doctor, Doctor, I think a killer
  bee is circling me all the time!
DOCTOR: Oh, that's just a bug that's going
  around.

AMBULANCE DRIVER: Have an accident?
VICTIM: No, thanks, I just had one.

AMBULANCE DRIVER: Didn't you see the sign
  that said DON'T WALK?
VICTIM: I thought it was an ad for taxicabs.

Which Doctor?

What flies on a broom and carries a
medicine bag?
  A *witch doctor*.

WITCH DOCTOR (to sick native): Drink this potion of ground bat wing, lizard tail, alligator scale, and hawk feathers.

SICK NATIVE: I drank that yesterday and it didn't work.

WITCH DOCTOR: Okay, take two aspirins and call me in the morning.

MOTHER CANNIBAL (to witch doctor): I'm worried about Junior. He wants to be a vegetarian.

The doctor told his new patient, "You're in fine shape. You should live to be eighty."

"But I am eighty!" the patient exclaimed.

"See?" said the doctor. "What did I tell you?"

PATIENT: I've got a pain in my left leg.

DOCTOR: (after examination): There's nothing I can do for you. It's old age.

PATIENT: But my left leg is just as old as my right leg and that one feels fine!

PATIENT: I have a weak back.

DOCTOR: When did you notice it?

PATIENT: Oh, about a week back.

PATIENT: You were right, Doctor, when you said you'd have me on my feet and walking around in no time.

DOCTOR: I'm happy to hear it. When did you start walking?

PATIENT: Right after I sold my car to pay your bill.

14

Famous Firsts

What figures do the most walking?
Roman numerals.

What invention allows people to walk
through walls?
Doors.

Say These
Three Times
Quickly

Frankenstein
feasted on flaming
fish at the free fish fry.

Frankenstein flies through fog and frost to fight flu fast.

Frankenstein threw three free throws.

The flimsy phantom fled the flood-filled flat.

Faint phantoms fear fat flat flounders.

What goes through water but doesn't get wet?
A ray of light.

When is a horse not a horse?
When it turns into a pasture.

Where do the people of India go for bagels?
To the New Delhi.

How are potatoes like loyal friends?
They're always there when the chips are down.

A scientist invented a liquid that would dissolve anything it touched. However, he couldn't sell the invention. Why?
There was nothing he could put the liquid in.

A scientist invented the most powerful glue in the world. However, he couldn't use it. Why?
He couldn't get the lid off the container.

Why are poets so poor?
Because rhyme doesn't pay.

When is a person not a person?
When he's a little cross.

What happened when the prisoners put on a play?

It was a cell-out.

Did you hear about the latest Dr. Jekyll and Mr. Hyde miracle medicine that was discovered?

One sip and you're a new man.

How can you live eighty years but only have twenty birthdays?

Be born on February 29.

What snacks should you serve robots at parties?

Assorted nuts and bolts.

What do squirrels give each other on Valentine's Day?

Forget-me-nuts.

Criss Cross

What would you get if you crossed . . .

. . . a shark with a parrot?
An animal that talks your ear off.

. . . a homing pigeon with a parrot?
A bird that asks the way home if it gets lost.

. . . a canary and a parrot?
A bird that knows both the words and the music.

. . .a bumblebee with a parrot?
An animal that talks about how busy it is all the time.

. . . a hyena with a parrot?
An animal that laughs at its own jokes.

. . . a woodpecker with a parrot?
An animal that talks to you in Morse code.

. . . a parrot and a soldier?
A parrot-trooper.

What kind of TV program is shown early in the morning?
A breakfast serial.

What is the favorite meal of a shipbuilder?
Launch-time.

If two shirt collars had a race, who would win?
Neither. It would end in a tie.

Why was the belt arrested?
For holding up the pants.

What kind of running means walking?
Running out of gas.

What does a computer call its mother and father?
Mama and Data.

What's the Difference?

What's the difference between a comedian and a gossip?

A comedian has a sense of humor; a gossip has a sense of rumor.

What's the difference between a rug and a bottle of medicine?

One you take up and shake, the other you shake up and take.

What's the difference between the law and an ice cube?

One is justice, and the other is just ice.

What's the difference between the North Pole and the South Pole?

All the difference in the world.

What's the difference between a frog and a cat?

A frog croaks all the time, the cat only nine times.

What's the difference between the sun and a loaf of bread?
One rises from the east, the other from the yeast.

Why did the motorist put a rabbit in her gas tank?
Because she needed the car for short hops.

Did you hear the joke about the sun?
Never mind, it's way over your head.

What happens when the sun gets tired?
It sets awhile.

What flower do you get if you cross a pointer and a setter?
A poinsettia.

What did the boy
     snake say to the girl snake?

"Give me a little hiss."

Why are four-legged animals such poor
dancers?
   *You would be, too, if you had two left
   feet.*

Why is 3 + 3 = 7 like your left foot?
   It's not right.

How do you make meat loaf?
   Send it on vacation.

How is an escaping prisoner like an
airplane pilot?
   They both want safe flights.

What likes to spend the summer in a fur coat and the winter in a wool bathing suit?
  A moth.

Why did the burglar take a bath before breaking out of jail?
  To make a clean getaway.

Why did Dracula go to the orthodontist?
To improve his bite.

What's the
difference
between
electricity and
lightning?
*You have
to pay for
electricity.*

What did the electric company say during
the blackout?
"AC come, AC go!"

What did the locksmith do when his shop caught on fire?

He made a bolt for the door.

Why did the knife sharpener quit his job?

He couldn't take the grind.

Why do bakers always want dough?

Because they knead it.

What makes a road broad?

The letter B.

What punctuation mark is used in writing dance music?

A polka dot.

What do you have in December that you don't have in any other month?

The letter D.

Whose figure can't be seen?

A figure of speech.

What does it mean when the barometer is falling?

It means that whoever nailed it up didn't do such a good job.

What's the best way to keep your food bills down?

Use a heavier paperweight.

Who grows cucumbers for a pickle factory?

The farmer in the dill.

What would you call it if the cow that jumped over the moon fought Taurus the bull?

Steer wars.

Why don't cows ever have any money?
Because the farmer milks them dry.

Why was the farmer arrested in the morning?
Because he hit the hay the night before.

What kind of cattle are always broke?
Bum steers.

Why did the otter cross the road?
  To get to the otter side.

Why did the whale cross the ocean?
  To get to the other tide.

Why did the banana go out with the prune?
  Because it couldn't get a date.

What salad do people prefer when they want privacy?
  Lettuce alone.

What did the criminal say when he was saved from the hangman at the last minute?
  "No noose is good news."

What's a comedian's favorite food?
  Cream of wit.

Why did the angry man put a firecracker
under his pancakes?
He wanted to blow his stack.

What bird is useful in boxing matches?
Duck.

15

Wacky Insults: I Love Monkeys, Too

I love you,
I love you,
I love you, I do—
But don't get excited—
I love monkeys, too.

Roses are red,
Violets are blue,
Oatmeal is mushy,
And so are you.

Roses are red,
Violets are blue,
A monkey like you,
Belongs in the zoo.

The rain makes everything beautiful.
It makes the flowers blue;
But if the rain makes everything
    beautiful,
Why doesn't it rain on you?

Roses are red,
Grass is green,
Your ears are cute—
But there's nothing between.

I have you in my heart,
I have you in my liver.
If I had you in my arms,
I'd throw you in the river.

Roses are red,
Noses are blue,
Pickles are sour,
And so are you.

Good morning to you,
Good morning to you
You look very drowsy,
In fact, you look lousy,
Is that any way
To start out the day?

172

Roses are red,
Napoleon's dead.
Barrels are empty,
And so is your head.

There are rocks in the ocean,
There are rocks in the sea,
But how the rocks got in your head
Is a puzzle to me.

Your father is a baker,
Your mother cuts the bread,
And you're the little doughnut
With a hole right through your
    head.

Roses are red,
Violets are blue,
Umbrellas get lost,
Why don't you?

Roses are red,
Violets are blue,
Sidewalks are cracked,
And so are you.

Roses are red,
Violets are blue.
I was born human,
What happened to you?

I wish I had your picture,
It would be very nice.
I'd hang it in the attic,
To scare away the mice.

Roses are red,
Pickles are green.
My face is a holler
But yours is a scream.

Your head is like a ball of straw,
Your nose is long and funny,
Your mouth is like a cellar door,
But I still love you, honey.

16

Weird Characters

Two giants are standing on a bridge. One is the father of the other's son. What relation are the two giants?
Husband and wife.

Why is a zombie a poor liar?
Because it's a dead giveaway.

What room does a zombie stay out of?
The living room.

Are there any blond zombies?
Well, they're not born blond, but they dye that way.

Where do they send young werewolves
who won't behave properly?
  To obedience school.

FETCH!

How do werewolves study?
  They paw over their books.

Which side of a werewolf has the most hair?
  The outside.

What kind of story does a gravedigger like?
  One with a cemetery plot.

What's the Difference?

What's the difference between a werewolf and a flea?
  A werewolf can have fleas, but a flea can't have werewolves.

What's the difference between a hungry werewolf and a greedy werewolf?
  One longs to eat, and the other eats too long.

What's the difference between a werewolf and a comma?
  A werewolf has claws at the end of its paws; a comma has a pause at the end of its clause.

A Martian spaceship crashed in the desert. The pilot and his copilot escaped without injury. After looking over their damaged ship, however, they were discouraged.

"We'll never get back home to Mars," sobbed the Martian copilot. "Our ship is useless. Our engines are smashed. What are we going to do?"

"Don't panic," said the pilot. "We'll figure something out. After all, four heads are better than one."

Why are dragons not to be believed?
Because they're full of hot air.

Why do monsters forget so easily?
Because everything goes in one ear and out the others.

What's gray and prevents forest fires?
Smokey the Shark.

In what way is a monster good-looking?
Away off.

Why do witches fly brooms?
Because vacuum cleaners don't have long enough cords.

What kind of jewelry do witches wear on their wrists?
Charm bracelets.

What piece of jewelry frightens off a vampire?

A *ring* around the collar.

Why is an evil witch like a candle?

They are both wick-ed.

What awful creature can be found in many lunch boxes?

Sandwiches.

Where do you buy an extinct animal?

In a dino-store.

What does a monster do before he gets out of his car?

He kills the engine.

If you saw the Frankenstein monster standing on a handkerchief, how could you get the handkerchief without being in danger?

Wait until he walked away.

Why do skeletons catch cold faster than other creatures?

They get chilled to the bone.

How can you make two vampires out of one?

Tell it a monster joke and it will double up with laughter.

Why did the werewolf get a job as a comedian?

Because he was a howl.

What play by Shakespeare makes monsters cry?

Romeo and Ghouliet.

What do werewolves call a fur coat?

"Darling."

Now You See Him . . .

NURSE: Doctor, there's an invisible man in the waiting room.

DOCTOR: Tell him I can't see him.

What does the Invisible Man drink with cookies?

Evaporated milk.

What kind of children would the Invisible
Man and Woman have?
  *I don't know, but they wouldn't be much
  to look at.*

If the Invisible Man went
into space, what would he
be called?
  An astro-naught.

TV ANNOUNCER: Because
of the following special
program, the Invisible
Man will not be seen
tonight . . .

How does the Invisible
Man look?
  *Like nothing you ever
  saw.*

Why is the Invisible Man a poor liar?
Because anyone can see right through him.

What's more invisible than the Invisible Man?
His shadow.

What does the Invisible Man call his mother and father?
His transparents.

What did the Frankenstein monster say to the scarecrow?
"I can beat the stuffing out of you."

What does a skeleton serve her dinner on?
Bone china.

How can you make a witch scratch?
Take away her W.

What do evil witches have for dessert at Chinese restaurants?
Misfortune cookies.

What kind of dates do ghouls go out with?
Anybody they can dig up.

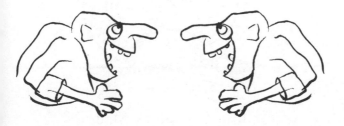

17

Loony Limericks: Sad Stories

At a bullfight in sunny Madrid
A tourist went clean off his lid.
  He made straight for the bull,
  While the crowd yelled, "The fool
Will go home on a slab!"—and he did.

There was a young woman named
    Gail
Who fancied she'd go for a sail.
    Well, she boarded the yacht,
    But she stayed on her cot,
'Cept when she hung over the rail.

An odd fellow from Ecuador
Had the same shape behind as before.
    They did not know where
    They should offer a chair,
So he had to sit down on the floor.

A painter who lived in Great Britain
Interrupted two girls from their
    knittin'.
    He said with a sigh,
    "That park bench—well, I
Just painted it, right where you're
    sittin'."

There was an old woman of Thrace
Whose nose spread all over her face.
  She got very few kisses;
  The reason for this is
There wasn't a suitable place.

There was a young girl from Bryn
    Mawr
Who carried politeness too far.
  "Don't look now," she said,
  With a tilt of her head,
"But someone is stealing your car!"

There was a young girl in the choir
Whose voice went up higher and
    higher.
  It reached such a height,
  It was clear out of sight;
And they found it next day in the
    spire.

A daring young fellow in Bangor
Sneaked a huge jet from its hangar.
  When he crashed in the bay,
  Neighbors laid him away
Much more in sorrow
      than anger.

Said a gentle old man, "I suppose
I ought not to wear my best clothes.
  But what can I do?
  I have only two,
And these are no better than those."

A thrifty young fellow of Shoreham
Made brown paper trousers and wore
   'em.
  He looked nice and neat
  Till he bent in the street
To pick up a pin, then he tore 'em.

A greedy young actress once said,
As she gobbled down slices of bread,
  "If I eat one more crust,
  I'm sure I will bust"—
At which point her audience fled.

18

Grab Bag

What kind of book tells you about all the different kinds of owls?
Who's Whoo.

What nationality are people from the Arctic Circle?

North Polish.

How do you get through a patch of poison ivy?

You itch-hike.

Criss Cross

What would you get if you crossed . . .

. . . a skunk and a raccoon?

A *dirty look from the raccoon.*

. . . a telephone and a shirt?

Ring around the collar.

. . . a galaxy and a toad?

Star warts.

. . . an airplane, an automobile, and a dog?
  A flying car-pet.

. . .a watch and four cups of milk?
  A quartz watch.

. . . a rabbit and a lawn sprinkler?
  Hare spray.

. . . a canary and an elephant?
  A pretty messy cage.

What's the Difference?

What's the difference between a zoo and a delicatessen?

A zoo has a man-eating tiger, and a delicatessen has a man eating salami.

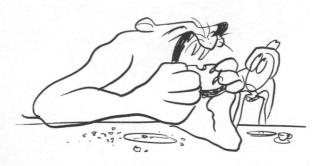

What's the difference between an animal losing his hair and a person painting a small building?

One sheds his coat, the other coats his shed.

Say These Three Times Quickly

Most ghosts prefer preshrunk sheets.

Good blood, bad blood.

The shark ate each sixth chick on the stick.

The shark shocked seven short soldiers. Now, if the shark shocked seven short soldiers, where are the seven short soldiers the shark shocked?

Mrs. Smith's Fish Sauce Shop.

Sign on a Freshly Painted Park Bench

WATCH IT OR WEAR IT

Knock-knock.
  Who's there?
Sanyo.
  Sanyo who?
What's Sanyo mind?

Knock-knock.
  Who's there.
Datsun, Honda, and Toyota.
  Datsun, Honda, and Toyota who?
Datsun old knock-knock joke and
I Honda-stand Toyota be a law
against it.

Scratch-scratch.
  Who's there?
Hurd and Kent.
  Hurd and Kent who?
Hurd my hand so I Kent knock
anymore!

Why did the prisoner stuff himself with candies and sweets?
He wanted to break out.

Lem and Clem were walking along the railroad tracks. Lem saw a man's leg. "I think that's Joe's leg," he said.

Then they saw a body. "I think that's Joe's body," said Clem.

Walking on, they came to a head. Lem picked it up and started shaking it.

"Hey, Joe!" he said in a worried voice. "Joe—are you hurt?"

Where do rivers sleep?
In riverbeds.

The Parents of Us All

What is the earliest known fruit?
Adam's apple.

Why was Adam's first day so long?
Because there was no Eve.

Who was the first nuclear scientist in history?

Eve. She knew all about Atom.

What did Eve do when she wanted sugar for her coffee?

She raised Cain.

A greedy young lady of Eden
On apples was quite fond of feedin'.
  She gave one to Adam,
  Who said, "Thank you, madam,"
And then they were kicked out of
    Eden.

How did Adam and Eve feel when they left the Garden of Eden?

Put out.

$\underline{\overline{19}}$

Don't Be Silly!

Say These Three Times Quickly

The wretched witch watched a walrus washing. Did the wretched witch watch a walrus washing? If the wretched witch watched a walrus washing, where's the washing walrus the wretched witch watched?

The ghost goes by Blue Goose bus.

Monsters chomp cheap cherry marshmallows.

The shark shops for short silk shorts.

The shark slashes sheets.

Why doesn't a frog jump when it's sad?
It's too unhoppy.

What happened to the pelican that stuck his head into a wall socket?
He now has an electric bill.

What would happen if you cut your left side off?

You'd be all right.

What did the bored cow say as she got up in the morning?

"Just an udder day."

Why did the cow go to the psychiatrist?

Because it had a fodder complex.

Why are undertakers like true friends?

They are the last ones to let you down.

Why is doing nothing so tiring?

Because you can't stop and rest.

What did the surgeon say to the patient who complained about his operation?

"Next time, suture self!"

Why are executioners so understanding?
Because they quickly get the hang of things.

What made the farmer yell?
Someone stepped on his corn.

When does a lion relax?
When it's lion down.

Criss Cross

What would you get if you crossed . . .

. . . a doctor and a clock?
  A tick doc.

. . . a clock and a porcupine?
  A stickler for punctuality.

. . . a small horn and a little flute?
A tootie flooty.

. . . a crocodile and an abalone?
A crocabalone.

What do Eskimos get under their eyes
when they can't sleep?
Arctic Circles.

What stretcher can't carry sick people?
A rubber band.

Who is safe when a
man-eating lion is on
the loose?
*Women and
children.*

"What Did You Say?"

What did the sock say to
the foot?
  "You're putting me on."

What did one stocking say
to the other stocking?
  "So long now, I gotta run."

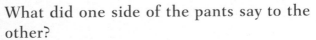

What did one side of the pants say to the
other?
  "Let's split!"

How much birdseed should you get for a
quarter?
  None. Quarters don't eat birdseed.

What key do cattle sing in?
  Beef-flat.

What's the easiest way to count cows?
On a cow-culator.

What can you swallow that can also
swallow you?
Water.

What happened to the thin woman after
she swallowed the thermometer?
She gained weight by degrees.

What can you find in the Great Wall of China that the Chinese never put there?
Cracks.

What drink is popular among monsters?
Ghoul-Aid.

Why does Dr. Jekyll go south in winter?
To tan his Hyde.

What's green and goes slam, slam, slam, slam?
A four-door pickle.

How do you spell pickle backward?
P-I-C-K-L-E B-A-C-K-W-A-R-D.

What phrase is heard most often at pickle card games?
"Dill me in."

Time on Their Hands

What goes "chit-chat, tick-tock, boom-gong"?
A sick clock.

What happens to people who steal watches?
The lawyer gets the case and the judge gives them time.

Why did the silly kid put his watch on the scale?
To see if it was gaining or losing time.

Who invented the grandfather clock?
Pendulum Franklin.

Why does time fly?
To get away from all the people who are trying to kill it.

What did the digital watch say to its mother?
"Look, Ma, no hands!"

Can February March?
No, but April May.

What does a banana do when it sees a gorilla?
The banana splits.

What's raised during the rainy season in Brazil?
Umbrellas.

Who talks for the workers in a bicycle factory?

A spokesperson.

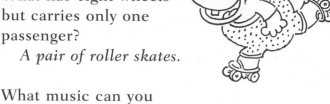

What has eight wheels but carries only one passenger?

A pair of roller skates.

What music can you play with your shoes?

Sole music.

What instrument does a lighthouse keeper play?

The foghorn.

What is every American president's occupation?

Cabinetmaker.

What's found on the cover of a monster beauty magazine?

A cover ghoul.

Why didn't the fireplace burn too well?

Because its hearth wasn't in it.

What did the big skillet say to the little skillet?

"Hiya, small fry!"

What's the best way to buy holes?

Wholesale.

Which member of the ship's crew puts away the playing cards?

The deckhand.

What's the best way to carve wood?

Whittle by whittle.

20

African Safari

What's gray, carries flowers, and cheers you up when you're sick?

A get-well-ephant.

Name ten African animals in three seconds?
Nine elephants and a giraffe.

Why do elephants get jobs at the ballpark?
Because they work for peanuts.

PATIENT: Can a person be in love with an elephant?
PSYCHIATRIST: Impossible!
PATIENT: Do you know anyone who wants to buy a very large engagement ring?

How much does a psychiatrist charge an elephant?
A hundred dollars for the visit and a thousand dollars for the couch.

Why do elephants lie down?
Because they can't lie up.

How do you keep an elephant from going through the eye of a needle?

Tie a knot in its tail.

What's worse than an elephant with an earache?

A giraffe with a sore throat.

Does a giraffe get a sore throat when its feet get wet?

Yes, but not until two weeks later.

Why are giraffes so slow to apologize?

It takes a long time for them to swallow their pride.

What do you call it when a bunch of giraffes try to get past each other on a narrow street?

A gi-raffic jam.

Jerome was a silly giraffe
Who wore a disguise for
    a laugh.
  Well, Jerome was
  too tall
  (or the costume too small).
Did it cover Jerome? Only half!

What do doctors give elephants to calm them down?

Trunk-quilizers.

An elephant lay in his bunk.
In slumber his chest rose and sunk.
  He snored and he snored
  Till the jungle folks roared—
And his wife tied a knot in his trunk.

Why are elephants so smart?
Because they have lots of gray matter.

What did the elephant say when it sat on the box of cookies?
"That's the way the cookie crumbles."

What do you get if you cross an elephant
and a jar of peanut butter?
You get a peanut butter sandwich that
never forgets.

There was a young lady from Niger,
Who smiled as she rode on a tiger.
    They came back from a ride
    With the lady inside,
And a smile on the face of the tiger.

How many different kinds of gnus are there?

Two kinds: good gnus and bad gnus.

LEM: What's a polygon?
CLEM: A missing parrot.

What does Tarzan sing at Christmastime?

"Jungle Bells."

21

Loony Limericks: Chuckles & Snickers

A clergyman read from his text
How Samson was scissored and vexed.
  Then a barber arose
  From his sweet summer doze,
Got rattled, and shouted, "Who's next?"

The wife of the butcher of Clewer
Was riding a bike and it threw her.
   The butcher came by
   And said, "Dearest, don't cry,"
And he fastened her on with a skewer.

A man of terrific physique
Took a bath every day in a creek,
   Till one day it ran dry.
   Then he said with a sigh,
"Call the plumber! This thing's sprung
    a leak!"

There was a young maid of Manila
Whose favorite ice cream was vanilla.
   But sad to relate,
   Though you piled up her plate,
'Twas impossible ever to fill her.

There was a young man so benighted
He never knew when he was slighted.
  He'd go to a party,
  And eat just as hearty
As if he'd been really invited.

A kindly old lady once said
To a thief she found under her bed,
  "So near to the door,
  And so close to the floor,
I'm afraid you'll catch cold in your
    head."

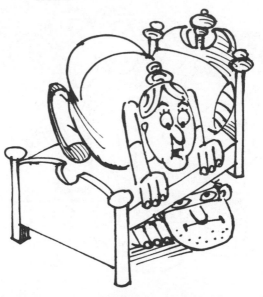

There was a young lady of Spain
Who hiccuped while riding a train,
  Not once, but again
  And again and again,
And again and again and again!

Two maidens were seated at tea
Discussing the things that might be.
  "I think I'll wed Willie,"
  Said Mollie to Millie,
"That is, if he asks me, you see."

There once was a pretty young thing
Who, when somebody asked her to
     sing,
  Replied, "Isn't it odd?
  I can never tell 'God
Save the Weasel' from 'Pop Goes the
     King'!"

The lazy old vicar of Bray
Allowed all his flowers to decay.
  His wife, more alert,
  Bought a powerful squirt,
And said to her spouse, "Let us spray."

There was a young lady of Flint
Who had a most horrible squint.
  She would scan the whole sky
  With her uppermost eye,
While the other was reading small
    print.

A careless zookeeper named Blake
Fell into a tropical lake.
  Said a fat alligator,
  A few minutes later,
"That's nice but I still prefer steak."

A hippo from Chesapeake Bay
Decided to take up ballet.
   So she stood on her toes
   And said, "Okay, here goes!"
And she made a big splash—on
      Broadway.

A canner, exceedingly canny,
One morning remarked to his granny,
  "A canner can can
  Anything that he can,
But a canner can't can a can, can he?"

There was an old fellow named Cass
Who had all his pants made of brass.
  When I asked, "Do they chafe?"
  He said, "Yes, but I'm safe
Against pinches,
  and snakes
    in the grass."

22

Wacky Insults: You Got Me!

"I'm a bookworm."

"Oh, I thought you were just the ordinary kind."

You must be the head kid on the block—the blockhead.

"What, in your opinion, do you consider the height of stupidity?"

"How tall are you?"

"Do you believe it's possible to communicate with dumb animals?"

"Yes, I can understand you distinctly."

You look like you're walking around just to save on funeral expenses.

You could be arrested for impersonating a garbage can.

"Have you heard the story about the dirty shirt?"

"No."

"Well, that's one on you!"

"Look at me when I'm talking."
   "I'd rather not. I have my own problems."

A crumb like you should have stayed in bread.

"How is your health these days?"
   "I sleep soundly and eat like a horse."
   "Please leave your manners out of this."

Have you ever thought of checking into the home for the chronically strange?

"There are hundreds of ways of making money, but only one honest way."

"What's that?"

"Aha! I knew you wouldn't know!"

"You look like George Washington."

"Is it my eyes, my nose, or my high brow?"

"No, it's your wig."

"A little bird whispered something in my ear."

"It must have been a cuckoo."

"Did you make up that joke all by yourself?"

"Yes, out of my head."

"You must be."

"If a person's brain stops working, does he die?"

"How can you ask such a question? You're alive, aren't you?"

You might as well laugh at yourself once in a while— everyone else does.

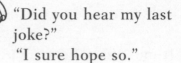

"Did you hear my last joke?"

"I sure hope so."

"What's the idea of telling everyone that I'm stupid?"

"Sorry, I didn't realize it was a secret."

"My mind seems to wander."

"Don't worry. It's too weak to go very far."

"Want to lose ten pounds of ugly fat?"

"Sure."

"Cut off your head."

"How many lumps will you have in your tea?"

"None. I don't like lumpy tea."

"Keep still. I'm trying to think."
    "Experimenting again?"

"You've got to admit I'm always trying."
    "Yes, you most certainly are."

"I've got an idea."
    "Be good to it; it must be lonely."

"Do you know what your
one great fault is?"
    "I can't imagine."
    "Right, only I never
expected you to admit it."

"Why do you wear
eyeglasses?"
    "Because my eyes are weak."
    "Have you thought about
wearing a glass hat?"

"Your feet are like your voice."

"How's that?"

"Both are flat."

"There were eight morons: do, re, fa, sol, la, ti, do."

"Hey, what about mi?"

"Sorry, I forgot about you."

23

Bloopers & Snoopers

Say These Three Times Quickly

The monster muddled the middle melody.

Selfish sharks sell shut shellfish.

Which wristwatch is a Swiss witch's wristwatch?

How do you get pies to work for the government?
Add the letter S. It makes pies spies.

What makes potatoes good detectives?
They keep their eyes peeled.

Why can't you trust fishermen and shepherds?
Because they live by hook and by crook.

Why can't a man living in New York City be buried west of the Mississippi?
Because he's still alive.

How do you find a missing barber?
Comb the city.

What happens if you cross a goat and a lion?
You have to get a new goat.

What has a soft bed but never sleeps, and a big mouth but never speaks?
A river.

What was the tow truck doing at the auto race?
Trying to pull a fast one.

Criss Cross

What would you get if you crossed . . .

. . . poison ivy with a four-leaf clover?
A rash of good luck.

. . . a potato and a sponge?
  A vegetable that soaks up lots of gravy.

. . . a penguin and a schoolteacher?
  A formal education.

. . . a small fish and a Russian ruler?
  A czardine.

~~~

If two authors sued each other, what would you have?
  A bookcase.

Why do some fishermen use helicopters to get their bait?
  Because the whirlybird gets the worm.

What kind of case would a lawyer have who slipped and hurt himself at the pool?
  A bathing suit.

What kind of car does
a rich rock star drive?
*A Rock and Rolls-
Royce.*

What do you find in
air-conditioned banks?
Cold cash.

Why do bankers go to
art school?
*They like to draw
interest.*

What's a banker's favorite dance?
The vaults.

What do sweet potatoes do when they play
together?
They have yam sessions.

Who can't get his part straight even with a comb and a brush?
A *bad actor.*

What bird is not to be trusted?
A *stool pigeon.*

What kind of hawk has no wings?
A *tomahawk.*

What sort of person invents theories?
A *theory-ous one.*

How do you get fur from a bear?
By car, bus, train, or plane.

Why doesn't it pay to talk to anyone with four lips?
All you get is a lot of double talk.

What did the peel say to the banana?
"Don't move, I've got you covered."

Why was the weatherman arrested?
Because he was caught shooting the breeze.

How do you send a message to a Viking?
By Norse code.

What are the odds of something happening at 12:50 P.M.?
Ten to one.

Best-seller List

How to Live in the Swamp by Tad Pohl

Foot Problems by Aiken Bunyan

Primitive Warfare by Beau N. Arros

Polar Exploration by R. U. Cold and I. M. Freeson

What does an octopus wear?
   A coat of arms.

What kind of fish do they serve on airplanes?
   Flying fish.

Where do pilots keep their personal things?
In air pockets.

When is a man like a suit of clothes?
When his tongue has a coat and his breath comes in short pants.

Why are fish poor tennis players?
Because they don't like to get close to the net.

How does a deaf fish hear?
With a herring aid.

What's black and white and wrinkled and makes pit stops?

A racing prune.

What's round, purple, and orbits the sun?

The Planet of the Grapes.

What does a tuba call his father?

Ooom-papa.

A man opened a piece of furniture and a dozen people fell out. How could that be?

It was a missing persons' bureau.

What does a silly cow say when she's milked?

"Udder nonsense."

What do cows use for money?
Moola.

What close relatives do boy robots have?
Transistors.

What kind of cake holds water?
Sponge cake.

How can you tell German money?
By its marks.

What does a
lumberjack shout when
a tree falls too soon?
"Tim . . ."

What pigs write letters
to each other?
Pen pals.

How do you catch an electric eel?
With a lightning rod.

Why did the ding-dong wring his hands?
Because his bell was out of order.

What are Van Winkle
trousers?
Pants with a rip.

How do you make a pickle
laugh?
Tell it an elephant joke.

How do you
make an
elephant laugh?
Tell it a pickle joke.

What do you call a carpenter who misplaces his tools?
 A saw loser.

Why should you never mention the number 288 in front of the principal?
 Because it's two gross.

How mad can a kangaroo get?
 Hopping mad!

What does a match do when it loses its temper?
 It flares up.

What's the correct way to file an ax?
 Under the letter A.

Why is the letter D so aggravating?
 Because it makes Ma mad.

What's the quickest way to get ahead as an electrician?
Pull wires.

What kind of word could you take to tea parties?
A proper noun.

Why was the farmer angry?
Because someone got his goat.

What does an electric rabbit say?

"Watts up, Doc?"

How do most people learn to play the violin?

From scratch.

What does the voice of experience say?

"Ouch!"

What's the best way to improve a long speech?

Use shortening.

Why do demons and ghouls get along so well?

Because demons are a ghoul's best friend.

Why are bananas popular?

Because they have a-peel.

Is it all right to scream when the tailor presses your pants?
Yes, if you're still in them.

What kind of tea do the king and queen drink?
Royalty.

Where does success come before work?
In the dictionary.

24

All in the Family

A talkative fellow named Lister
Went walking one day with his sister.
  A bull at one poke
  Tossed her into an oak,
And 'twas six weeks before Lister
    missed her.

She was peeved and called him "Mr."
Not because he went and kr.,
  But because, just before,
  As she opened the door,
This same Mr. kr. sr.

FATHER: Why does Junior have so many
  holes in his forehead?
MOTHER: He's learning to eat with a fork.

"Now, Junior, apologize at once for saying
Mrs. Smith is ugly."
  "I'm sorry, Mrs. Smith, that you're ugly."

JUNIOR: Give me a cookie.
MOTHER: What's the magic word, dear?
JUNIOR: Hocus-pocus?

What do you call a baby rifle?
  A son of a gun.

What did the mother broom say to her broom infant?

"Go to sweep, little baby."

A baby in Kalamazoo
Remarked quite distinctly, "Goo-goo."
  'Twas explained by his ma,
  And likewise his pa,
That he meant to say, "How do you do?"

There was a young man from Angora
Who married—for richer or poorer.
  He'd not been long wed
  When he fell out of bed
And said, "Drat, I have married a
    snorer!"

What does a proud computer call his little son?

A microchip off the old block.

A very strange lad from Glasgow
Took all of his meals with his cow.
　　He explained, "It's uncanny—
　　She's so like Aunt Fanny!"
But he didn't indicate how.

Here lies a young salesman named
    Phipps,
Who married on one of his trips
    A widow named Block.
    He died of the shock
When he saw there were six little
    chips.

I said, "Perhaps," and that's final!

"Mom, can I go out and play?"
    "With those holes in your socks?"
    "No, with the kids next door."

When the baby cries at night, who gets up?
The whole neighborhood.

25

Loony Limericks: Moans & Groans

Despite his impressive physique,
Atlas was really quite meek.
  If a mouse showed its head,
  He would jump into bed
With a terrible bloodcurdling shriek.

A charming old lady named Gretel,
Instead of a hat, wore a kettle.
　　When they called her misguided,
　　She said, "I've decided
To show all the neighbors my mettle."

There was a young lady of Cork
Whose pa made a fortune in pork.
　　He bought for his daughter
　　A tutor who taught her
To balance green peas on her fork.

A newspaper reader named Gage
Would fly into a terrible rage
　　When he would choose
　　To read some big news
And find it continued . . .
　　　　next page!

A fellow named William John Lew
Got more hairy each year as he grew.
  Unable one day
  To shave it away,
He sighed, "Call me Winnie-the-Pooh!"

There was a young girl in Havana
Who slipped on a skin of banana.
  Away went her feet,
  And she took a seat
In a very unladylike manner.

A fellow who lived in New Guinea
Was known as a silly young ninny.
  He utterly lacked
  Good judgment and tact,
And as for clean socks—hadn't any!

A cheese that was aged and gray
Was walking and talking one day.
  Said the cheese, "Kindly note
  My mama was a goat
And I'm made out of curds, by the
    whey."

26

Wacky Insults: Hey, Waiter!

CUSTOMER: This soup isn't fit for a pig!
WAITER: I'll take it back sir, and bring you some that is.

CUSTOMER: I feel like a sandwich.
WAITER: Funny, you don't look like one.

"You look full."
    "How full?"
    "Aw-ful."

CUSTOMER: Waiter, how come this sandwich is squashed?
WAITER: You told me to step on it, didn't you?

"Waiter!"
    "Yes, sir?"
    "What is this?"
    "It's bean soup, sir."
    "I don't want to know what's been—what is it now?"

CUSTOMER: Hey, waiter! What kind of pie did you bring me? Are you sure this is apple pie?

WAITER: What does it taste like?

CUSTOMER: I don't know.

WAITER: Then what difference does it make?

WAITER: I have boiled tongue, fried liver, and pig's feet.

CUSTOMER: I'm not interested in your medical problems. Just bring me a cheese sandwich and coffee.

CUSTOMER: Waiter, do you have frog's legs?

waiter: Yes, sir.

CUSTOMER: Then why don't you hop into the kitchen and get me a doughnut and coffee?

CUSTOMER: What's the difference between the blue-plate special and the white-plate special?

WAITER: The white-plate special is ten cents extra.

CUSTOMER: Is the food any better?

WAITER: No, but we wash the dishes.

CUSTOMER: I'm giving a dinner for all my friends tonight.

WAITER: Oh—you must be the party that reserved a table for two.

CUSTOMER: I understand that fish is brain food.

WAITER: Yes, I eat it all the time.

CUSTOMER: Oh, well, there goes another scientific theory.

27

Famous Limericks

You will find by the banks of the Nile,
The haunts of the great crocodile.
He will welcome you in
With an innocent grin—
Which gives way to a satisfied smile.

A thoughtful old man of Lahore,
When a subject was getting a bore,
　　Would wisely arrange
　　Conversation to change
By falling in fits on the floor.

As a beauty I am not a star.
There are others more handsome by far;
　　But my face—I don't mind it,
　　For I am behind it;
It's the people in front that I jar.

There was an old man on whose nose
Most birds of the air could repose;
　　But they all flew away
　　At the close of the day,
Which relieved that old man and his
　　　nose.

There was an old lady of
France,
Who taught little ducklings
to dance;
When she said, "Tick-a-tack!"
They only said, "Quack!"
Which grieved that old lady of France.

Oh, I'm glad I'm protected from
knocks,
From my necktie clear down to my socks,
And padded and bolstered
Fenced-in and upholstered
With muscles to take up the shocks.

I'd rather have fingers than toes;
I'd rather have ears than a nose;
And as for my hair,
I'm glad it's all there:
I'll be awfully sad when it goes.

I'd rather have habits than clothes,
For that's where my intellect shows.
   And as for my hair
   Do you think I should care
To comb it at night with my toes?

I wish that my room had a floor;
I don't care very much for the door,
   But this walking around
   Without touching the ground
Is getting to be such a bore.

Said a foolish young lady of Wales,
"A smell of gas prevails."
   Then she searched with a light
   And later that night
Was collected—in seventeen pails.

An important young man of Quebec
Had to welcome the Duchess of Teck.
  So he bought for a dollar
  A very high collar
To save himself washing his neck.

There was an old person of Ware
Who rode on the back of a bear;
  When they said, "Does it trot?"
  He said: "Certainly not,
It's a Moppsikon Floppsikon bear."

There once was an old man of Brest
Who was always funnily dressed:
  He wore gloves on his nose
  And a hat on his toes,
And a boot in the middle of his chest.

"Well, well!" said the tortoise. "Dear
    me,
How defective your motor must be!
  Though I speed every day
  Not a fine do I pay;
The police cannot catch me, you see!"

Said the snail to the tortoise: "You may
Find it hard to believe what I say.
   You will think it absurd,
   But I give you my word,
They fined me for speeding today."

There was a young man of Quebec
Who was frozen in snow to his neck.
   When asked, "Are you friz?"
   He replied, "Yes, I is,
But we don't call this cold in Quebec."

There was an old man of Dumbree
Who taught little owls to drink tea;
  For he said, "To eat mice
  Is not proper or nice,"
That amiable man of Dumbree.

There was an old man of West Dumpet
Who possessed a large nose like a
    trumpet;
  When he blew it loud
  It astonished the crowd
And was heard through the whole of
    West Dumpet.

There once was a knowing raccoon
Who didn't believe in the moon.
  "Every month—don't you see—
  There's a new one," said he,
"No real moon could wear out so soon!"

There was once a man from Oporta
Who daily got shorter and shorter.
  The reason, he said,
  Was the hod on his head,
Which was filled with the heaviest
    mortar.

His sister named Lucy O'Finner
Grew constantly thinner and thinner.
    The reason was plain—
    She slept out in the rain,
And was never allowed any dinner.

There was an old fellow of Clewer,
Whose wife was as thin as a skewer.
    Last night, sad to say,
    She, at eight, "passed away"
Through the bars of a drain to the
        sewer.

To manage to keep up a brain
Is no easy job, it is plain;
    That's why a great many
    Don't ever use any,
Thus avoiding the care and the strain.

There was a young lady whose chin
Resembled the point of a pin;
  So she made it sharp,
  And purchased a harp,
And played several tunes with her
      chin.

There was an old man with a beard,
Who said, "It is just as I feared!—
　　Two owls and a hen,
　　Four larks and a wren,
Have all built their nests in my beard."

There was a young lady of Troy
Whom several large flies did annoy.
  Some she killed with a thump,
  Some she drowned at the pump
And some she took with her to Troy.

The chin it was meant to give trouble,
Either pimples or dimples or stubble,
  Though some have the gall
  To grow not at all,
While others come triple and
      double.

There once was a girl of New York
Whose body was lighter than cork.
  She had to be fed
  For six weeks upon lead
Before she went out for a walk.

There was a young man of Cadiz
Who inferred that life is what it is;
   For he had early learnt,
   If it were what it weren't
It could not be that which it is.

There was an old person of Fife
Who was greatly disgusted with life.
   They sang him a ballad,
   And fed him on salad,
Which cured that old person of Fife.

There was an old man of Sheerness
Who invited two friends to play chess,
   But he'd lent all the pieces
   To one of his nieces,
And stupidly lost the address.

28

Shake Well

How do you feel after a doctor sticks a needle into you?

Holier.

There once were some learned MDs
Who found a new kind of disease.
   They bottled and hawked it,
   And then they uncorked it
So thousands could catch it with ease.

Why aren't vampires welcome at the
bloodmobile?
   Because they only want to make
   withdrawals.

What gets twenty-five miles to a gallon of plasma?

A bloodmobile.

What would you get if you crossed a vampire with a doctor?

More blood tests than ever.

What Do They Come Down With?

What do dancers come down with?

Ballet-aches.

What do chimneys come down with?

The flu.

What does grass come down with?
   Hay fever.

What do motorcycle riders come down
with?
   Vroom-atism.

What does Mickey Mouse come down with?
   Disney spells.

What do beekeepers come down with?
   Hives.

Sign in the Window
of a Health Food Store

CLOSED ON ACCOUNT OF ILLNESS

What contains the most vitamins?
   A health food store.

DUKE: What did the doctor say was the matter with you?

LUKE: Asthma.

DUKE: Hey, Ma! What's the matter with Luke?

DOCTOR: Have you ever had that pain before?

PATIENT: Yes.

DOCTOR: Well, you've got it again.

Who wears a black cape, flies through the night, and wants to drink your blood?

A mosquito in a black cape.

DOCTOR: Do you know you have sixty thousand miles of blood vessels in your body?

PATIENT: No wonder I have tired blood.

What's the Difference?

What's the difference between a boxer and a person with a cold?

A boxer knows his blows; a person with a cold blows his nose.

What's the difference between a hill and a pill?

A hill is hard to get up; a pill is hard to get down.

What's the difference between a sick sailor and a blind man?

One can't go to sea; the other can't see to go.

Doctor, Doctor

PATIENT: Doctor, Doctor, I feel like a duck-doo!

DOCTOR: What's a duck-doo?

PATIENT: It goes quack quack!

PATIENT: Doctor, Doctor, I feel like an electric wire!

DOCTOR: How shocking!

PATIENT: Doctor, Doctor, I feel like a cup of coffee!

DOCTOR: Oh, perk up and don't be a drip!

PATIENT: Doctor, Doctor, I feel like a pack of cards!

DOCTOR: Shuffle off! I'll deal with you later.

PATIENT: Doctor, Doctor, I feel like a pogo stick!

DOCTOR: Sit down, sit down, sit down.

What's the Problem?

What was the Olympic athlete's problem?
Slipped discus.

What problem do you get from eating too much?

You get thick to your stomach.

NIP: How did you break your leg?
TUCK: See that hole over there?
NIP: Yes.
TUCK: Well, I didn't.

VISITOR: My friend was run over by a steamroller and he's in this hospital. What room is he in?
NURSE: Room 105, 106, 107, and 108.

29

Kooks & Spooks

What do ghouls wear on their feet in the rain?

Ghoul-oshes.

What does a werewolf put on at the beach?

Moon-tan lotion.

Why did the mad scientist cross a mole and Dick Tracy?

He wanted to bring law and order to the underground.

Five ghouls were sitting under an umbrella, but none of them got wet. How come?

It wasn't raining.

How does a skeleton study for a test?

It bones up for it the night before.

What do you call a skeleton that talks all the time?

A jawbone.

How does a book about a zombie begin?
With a dead-ication.

Why did the ghoul go to the beauty parlor?
It heard that was the place people went to dye.

What did the Frankenstein monster say when lightning struck him?
Nothing. He was too shocked.

What did the boy Frankenstein monster say to the girl Frankenstein monster?
"You are so electrocute."

What does a giant do when he breaks his big toe?

He calls a big toe truck.

How do monsters know they're in love?

When they love each shudder.

Criss Cross

What would you get if you crossed . . .

. . . a mummy with a stopwatch?

An old-timer.

. . . a newborn snake with a basketball?

A bouncing baby boa.

. . . a snake with a funeral?

A hiss and hearse.

. . . a monster with a Boy Scout?
  A monster that's always prepared.

. . . a ghost with an alligator?
  An animal that says "Boo" before it bites.

What ghost haunts a clock?
The spirit of the times.

How does a witch tell time?
With a witch-watch.

How does a werewolf file its claws?
Under the letter C.

Mr. Monster awoke at half past twelve
in a really terrible temper. "Where's my
supper?" he yelled at his wife. "Where are
my chains? Where's my poison? And where
are my—"

"Now, hold on," Mrs. Monster said.
"Can't you see I only have three hands?"

Why did the monster name both his sons
Ed?
Because two Eds are better than one.

What always follows a werewolf?
Its tail.

What is the Frankenstein monster's favorite piece of furniture?
An electric chair.

What happens if you don't pay your exorcist?
You get repossessed.

How do you help haunted eggs?
Get an eggs-orcist.

Mad About Martians

What did the Martian say to the gas pump?
"Take your finger out of your ear and listen to me!"

Where do Martians leave their spaceships?
  At parking meteors.

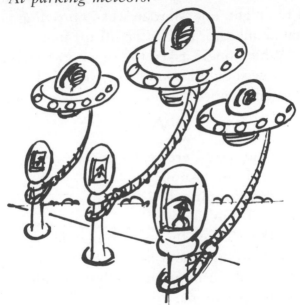

How do Martian cowboys signal each other?
  With communication saddle-lights.

Two Martians set their spaceship down in the wild swamp country of Florida. In the middle of the night, one Martian woke up yelling that an alligator had bitten off his foot.

"Which one?" asked the second Martian.

"How should I know?" the wounded Martian moaned. "They all look alike to me."

〰〰〰

SON: Dad, are there really ghosts?

FATHER: I don't know.

SON: Are vampires bad?

FATHER: I don't know.

SON: Do witches fly on broomsticks?

FATHER: I really can't say.

SON: You don't mind my asking you all these questions, do you?

FATHER: Not at all. How are you going to learn anything if you don't ask questions?

Where did extinct animals go for the summer months?

To the dino-shore.

Where do ghosts go for sun and fun?

To the sea-ghost.

Did you hear the joke about the fifty-foot giant?

Never mind—it's way over your head.

What instrument does a skeleton play?
  The trom-bone.

What do werewolves say on their
Christmas cards?
  "Best vicious of the season."

What's the hardest thing to sell a zombie?
  Life insurance.

Did you hear about the monster baby? He
was so ugly, his parents sent him back and
kept the stork.

The person who makes it does not need it.
The person who buys it does not use it.
The person who uses it does so without
knowing.
What is it?
  A coffin.

There was an old man in a hearse
Who murmured, "This might have
    been worse.
  Of course the expense
  Is simply immense,
But it doesn't come out of
    my purse."

What did Whistler's
Mother do when she
met the werewolf?
  *She went off her
  rocker.*

Why do witches feel
at home with turkeys?
  *Because a turkey is
  always a-gobblin'.*

What kind of money do monsters use?
  Weirdo.

When do monsters do well in school?
  When they use their heads.

How do you make a skeleton laugh?
  Tickle its funny bone.

How do you make a monster float?
Take two scoops of ice cream, some root beer, one large monster . . .

If one tyrannosaurus runs at fifteen miles per hour, and another tyrannosaurus runs at twenty-five miles per hour, what do you get if the two collide head-on?
Tyrannosaurus rex.

When are soldiers like people from outer space?
When they're Martian along.

Monster Sports

What's the monsters' favorite team?
The Giants.

Why couldn't the Frankenstein monster play basketball?
Because its sneakers were in the wash.

Where do dinosaurs race?
On dinosaur tracks.

What kind of dinosaur can you ride in a rodeo?
A bronco-saurus.

What kind of horses do zombies ride?
Nightmares.

～～～～～

Why are giants nice to have around?
They're a ton of fun.

Where do zombies swim?
In the Dead Sea.

When is a shark dizzy?
When its head is swimming.

How can you tell if you have a giant in
your bathtub?
You can't close the shower curtain.

Which branch of the service do werewolves join?
The Hair Force.

IGOR: How do you lead a werewolf?
BORIS: It's simple. First you get a rope. Then you tie it to the werewolf—
IGOR: And then?
BORIS: And then you find out where he wants to go.

FIRST MONSTER: My girlfriend has pedestrian eyes.
SECOND MONSTER: What are pedestrian eyes?
FIRST MONSTER: Eyes that look both ways before they cross.

If you see a monster chasing four men,
what time is it?
One after four.

Where would you
look for a lost
dinosaur after a
heavy rain?
In a dino-sewer.

What kind of mistake would it be if an
undertaker buried a body in the wrong
place?
A grave mistake.

What would you call a nervous witch?
A twitch.

On what kind of street does a zombie live?
A dead-end street.

What does a werewolf do when traffic is
snarled?

   It snarls back.

   Erasmus Emanuel Jones
Was awfully fond of grilled bones.
    After eating a score,
    He asked for some more—
That's why he lies under these stones.

There once was a man who said, "Oh,
Please, boa constrictor, let go!
    Don't you think that you can?"
    The snaked looked at the man,
And calmly responded, "Why, no!"

30

Loony Limericks: Help!

A singer they called Miss Diana
Was caught in a flood in Montana.
  She floated away,
   While her beau, so they say,
Accompanied her on the piana.

There once was a boy of Baghdad,
An inquisitive sort of a lad,
   Who said, "I will see
   If a sting has a bee."
Call the doctor! (He found that it
    had.)

I sat next to the duchess at tea.
'Twas just as I feared it would be!
   Her rumblings abdominal
   Were simply phenomenal,
And everyone thought it was me!

A luckless church tenor was Horace
Whose skin was so terribly porous,
   Sometimes in the choir
   He'd start to perspire,
And nearly drown out the whole
    chorus.

There was a young girl from Mobile
Who went up in a great Ferris wheel.
　When halfway around,
　She looked down at the ground
And it cost her a five-dollar meal.

There was a young lady of Michigan
To see her I never would wish again.
　She'd gobble ice cream
　Till with pain she would scream,
Then she'd order another big dish
　　again.

There once was a lady named Harris
That nothing would ever embarrass
　Till the powder she shook
　In the bath that she took
Turned out to be plaster of Paris.

A clumsy young soldier named Tom
Fell flat with a thousand-pound bomb.
  And now up on Mars
  They are saying, "My stars!
Where on Earth did you emigrate
    from?"

They say that ex-President Taft,
When hit by a golf ball, once laughed
  And said, "I'm not sore,
   But although he called 'Fore'
The place where he hit me was aft."

31

Let the Games Begin!

What's the best game to play when you've got the measles?

Hide-and-sick.

What did the jogger say when he ran into the doctor's office?

"*Ouch!*"

What has eighteen legs and red spots and catches flies?

A baseball team with the measles.

Why is a catcher's glove like the measles?

Both are catching.

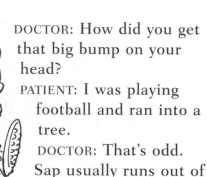

DOCTOR: How did you get that big bump on your head?

PATIENT: I was playing football and ran into a tree.

DOCTOR: That's odd. Sap usually runs out of a tree.

COACH: Are you hurt?

FOOTBALL PLAYER (moaning): I think so.
Better call me a doctor.

COACH: Okay, you're a doctor.

Sitting in her hospital bed, a hiker was bragging to the nurse about how she single-handedly took on a bear she met in the woods.

"So then, when I finally got my wrist firmly wedged between his teeth," she said, "I threw him down on top of me and started beating him senseless with my face."

What medical condition makes you run faster?

Athlete's foot.

Just because you've been off base all your life doesn't make you a baseball player.

You're in such bad shape, you get winded playing chess!

Where do they serve snacks to football players?
In the Soup-er Bowl.

Why is it hard to drive a golf ball?
Because it doesn't have a steering wheel.

Why was the baseball player asked to come along on the camping trip?
They needed someone to pitch the tent.

Why didn't anyone drink soda pop at the double-header baseball game?
Because the home team lost the opener.

Why did the jogger go to the vet?
Because his calves hurt.

Why do bakers make good baseball pitchers?

Because they know their batter.

Why didn't the first baseman get to dance with Cinderella?

Because he missed the ball.

What soccer player is never promoted?

The left back.

Why was the piano tuner hired to play on the baseball team?

Because he had perfect pitch.

How are judges like basketball referees?
They both work the courts.

Why don't baseball players join unions?
Because they don't like to be called out on strikes.

32

Plain Crazy

What happened when the police caught the frankfurter?
They grilled it.

Why did the cow jump over the moon?
Because the farmer had cold hands.

What's the saddest piece of clothing?
Blue jeans.

What's the saddest picture?
A blueprint.

What color is the wind?
Blew.

Criss Cross

What would you get if you crossed . . .

. . . an electric eel and a sponge?
Shock absorbers.

. . . a firefly with a reindeer?
Rudolph, the red-nosed firefly.

. . . an octopus with a mink?
A fur coat with too many sleeves.

. . . a giant and a skunk?
  A *big stink.*

. . . a cow and an elk?
  A *wonderful place to hang milk pails.*

What's better than a broken drum?
Nothing. It can't be beat!

What month is the worst for soldiers?
A long March.

What part of the body has the best social life?
Tonsils, because they get taken out so often.

What has become the most expensive vehicle to operate?
A shopping cart.

Who was the biggest monarch in history?
King Kong.

What's the best-looking geometric figure?
Acute angle.

How is a chicken stronger than an elephant?
An elephant can get chicken pox, but a chicken can't get elephant pox.

What can turn a lad into a lady?
The letter Y.

What room in a house is most dangerous
for men?

*The bathroom. That's where they have so
many close shaves.*

When is color fast?

When it doesn't run.

Who are the best letter writers?

*Fishermen. They'll always drop you a
line.*

What's quicker than a fish?
  The one who catches it.

What's the most noble creature in the sea?
  The Prince of Whales.

When doesn't a whale know what it's
talking about?
  When it spouts nonsense.

Where's the best place to see a man-eating
fish?
  In a seafood restaurant.

What kind of train has no wheels?
  A train of thought.

Why is a boat the cheapest form of
transportation?
  Because it runs on water.

How do you make metric coffee?
In the percoliter.

What travels around the earth without
using a single drop of fuel?
The moon.

What's faster than a speeding bullet, more
powerful than a locomotive—and green?
Superpickle!

What is a pickle's all-time favorite musical?
Hello, Dilly!

What beam weighs the least?
A light beam.

What's the most popular gardening
magazine?
The Weeder's Digest.

Best-seller List

Roller Coasters for Everyone by
   Lupe de Lupe

Astrology: What the Stars Mean by
   Horace Cope

Measuring Schoolwork by Tess D.
   Studenz

Stunt Driving for Fun,
   by E. Rex Carr

*How to Get 100 Things
   Free* by Fern Otten

Say These Three Times Quickly

King Kong coops up the cute cook.

The Abominable Snowman slays thirty-three sly, shy thrushes.

How many blocks could a blue blob break
if a blue blob could break blocks?

The skeleton shops at chop suey shops.

Sixty-six sticky skeletons.

33

How Dare You?

PATIENT: How long can a person live
without a brain?
DOCTOR: How old are you?

ADAM: I have a hoarse throat.
MADAM: Believe me, the resemblance
doesn't end there.

Doctor, Doctor

PATIENT: Doctor, Doctor, can I get rid of
fat where I have it most?
DOCTOR: Sure, but you'd look ridiculous
walking around without your head.

PATIENT: Doctor, Doctor, something is eating at my mind!

DOCTOR: Don't worry. It's sure to starve to death.

PATIENT: Doctor, Doctor, I'm getting more and more forgetful lately.

DOCTOR: When did you first notice this problem?

PATIENT: What problem?

PATIENT: Doctor, Doctor, a crate of eggs fell on my head!

DOCTOR: Well, the yolk's on you!

PATIENT: I know someone who thinks she's an owl.

DOCTOR: Who?

PATIENT: Now I know two people.

PATIENT: Tell me, what does the X ray of my head show?

DOCTOR: Nothing, I'm afraid.

PATIENT: If I stand on my head, all my blood rushes into it. Why doesn't all my blood rush into my feet when I stand on them?

DOCTOR: Your feet aren't empty.

If you had a brain transplant, the brain would reject you.

In your case, a brain operation would be minor surgery.

I hear you went to see a lot of doctors about your brain, but they couldn't find anything.

You're just what the doctor ordered—a pill!

Sick? Why, if they gave you a blood test, you'd fail.

You're so pale, the only way you could get color in your face is to stick your tongue out.

Before you decide to be a blood donor, make sure you're a blood owner.

You're in such bad shape, if a mosquito bit you, it would lose blood.

You're so anemic, if a mosquito bit you, all it would get is practice.

You remind me of medicine—thick, bitter, and hard to take.

No wonder the country's medical costs are so high. You make everyone sick.

MRS. SMITH: I just came from the doctor.
MRS. JONES: Which doctor?
MRS. SMITH: No, general practitioner.

If I took an aspirin, would you go away?

34

Raining Cats & Dogs

What doctor treats his patients like animals?

A vet.

When is a vet busiest?
When it rains cats and dogs.

When it rains cats and dogs, what does a vet step into?
Poodles.

A puppy whose hair was so flowing
There really was no way of knowing
    Which end was his head,
    Once stopped me and said,
"Please, sir, am I coming or going?"

There once were two cats in Kilkenny.
Each cat thought there was one too
        many,
    So they scratched and they fit
    And they tore and they bit,
Till instead of two—there weren't any.

What kind of royal cat do you find in a computer?

A Sir Kit.

What do you say to young dogs when they make a noise in a dog hospital?

"Hush, puppies!"

Where do they send homeless dogs?

To the arf-anage.

What sign do you see in front of a dog hospital?

NO BARKING ZONE

Doctor, Doctor

PATIENT: Doctor, Doctor, I think I'm a dog!
DOCTOR: Sit!

PATIENT: Doctor, Doctor, I think I'm a dog!
DOCTOR: How long has this been going on?
PATIENT: Ever since I was a puppy.

PATIENT: Doctor, Doctor, I think I'm a dog!
PSYCHIATRIST: Please lie down on the couch.
PATIENT: I can't. I'm not allowed on the furniture.

"For months I thought I was a dog, but my psychiatrist cured me."
  "How are you now?"
  "Fine. Feel my nose."

What happened after the dog swallowed a watch?

He got ticks.

Why did the silly kid try to feed pennies to his cat?

Because his mother told him to put his money in the kitty.

What color is a happy cat?
   Purr-ple.

How do you get milk from a cat?
   Steal its saucer.

How is cat food sold?
   So much purr can.

Criss Cross

What would you get if you crossed . . .

. . . a monster and a cat?
   A neighborhood without dogs.

. . . the Frankenstein monster with a hot dog?
   A Frankfurterstein.

. . . a cat and a parrot?
  A *purr-a-keet.*

35

The End

PATIENT: Doctor, doctor, nobody ever listens to me.
DOCTOR: Next!

How do you keep someone in suspense?
I'll tell you tomorrow.

How many bricks does it take to finish a house?
Only one—the last one.

What time is it when Dracula leaves his coffin?
Time to run.

What do tailors do when they get tired?
They just press on.

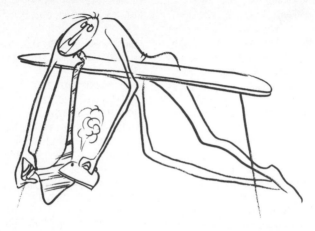

What part of a fish is like the end of a book?
The fin is.

Index

Limericks by Sheila Anne Barry, William Bellamy, B. G. Bourchier, Gelett Burgess, Lewis Carroll, Randall Davies, H. G. Dixey, Mary Mapes Dodge, Anthony Euwer, Mrs. Charles Harris, Oliver Herford, Oliver Wendell Holmes, Rudyard Kipling, Edward Lear, Cosmo Monkhouse, Walter Parke, J. H. Pitman, Langford Reed, Elsie Ridgewell, J. St. Loe Strachey, and Carolyn Wells